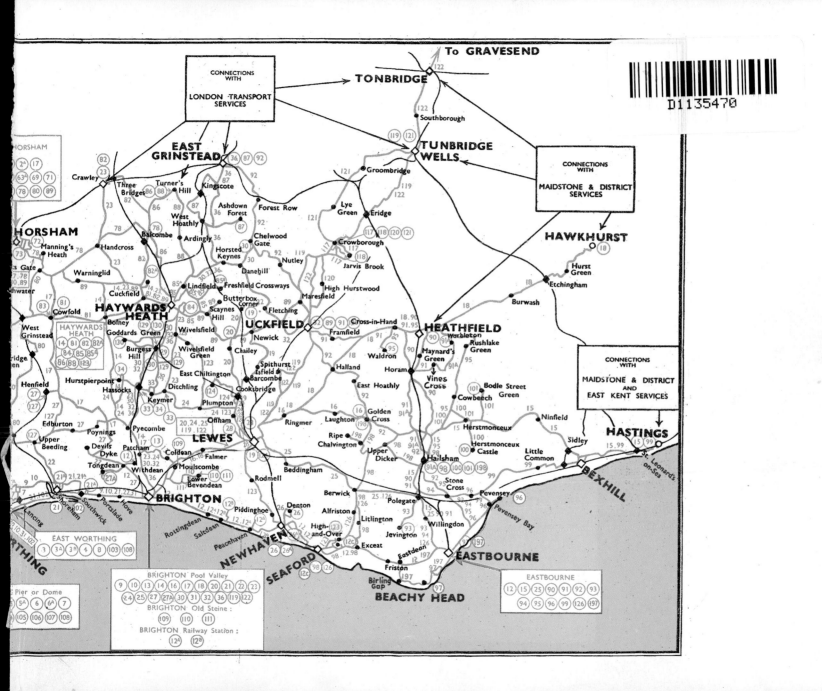

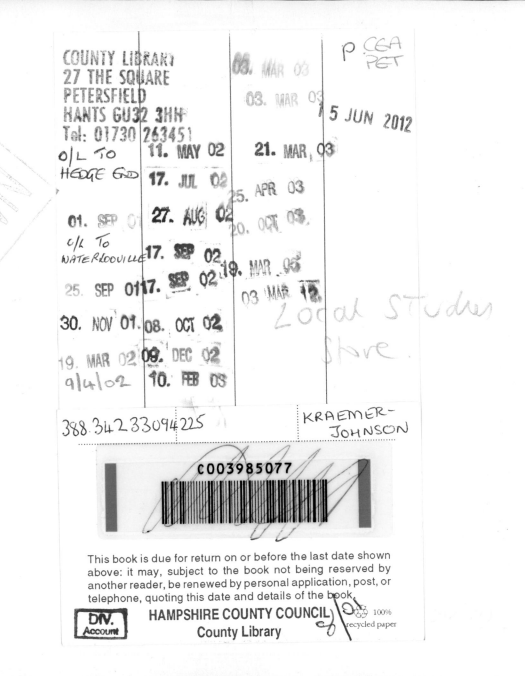

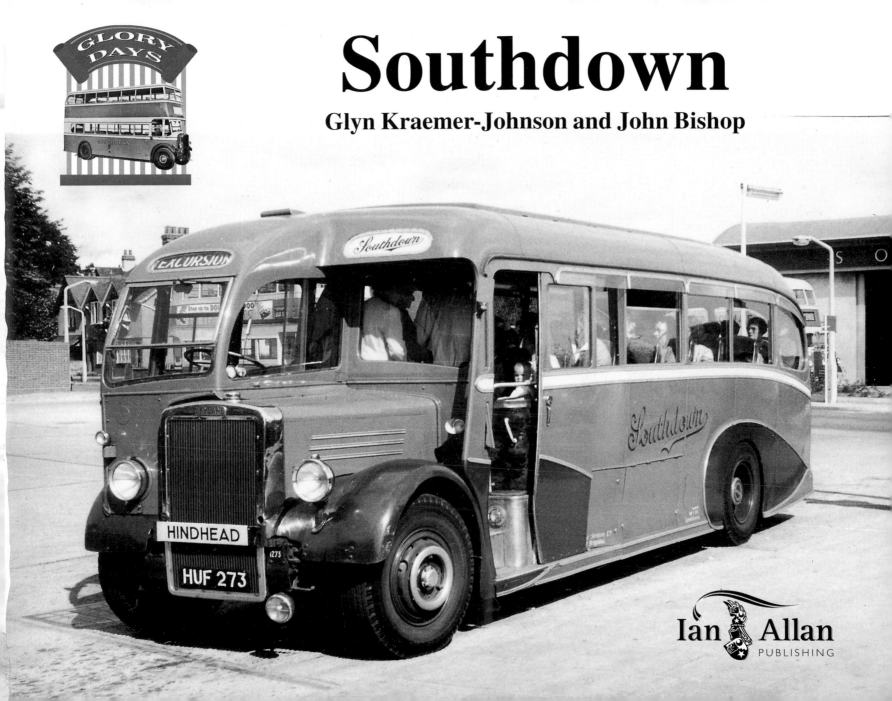

GLORY DAYS

Southdown

Glyn Kraemer-Johnson and John Bishop

Ian Allan PUBLISHING

Front cover:
The standard 'main road' double-deck chassis for most of the 'Fifties was the Leyland Titan PD2/12, which allowed the vehicle a width of 8ft. Initially Leyland bodywork was specified, but, when that manufacturer decided to cease its bodybuilding activities, 10 chassis were delivered with Northern Counties and gave the appearance of being altogether more substantial. No 764 (MUF 464) on the 22 route is seen about to leave Shoreham High Street bound inland towards Steyning and Midhurst. *Malcolm Keeping*

Back cover:
The Harrington Cavalier is possibly one of the most distinctive and individualistic coach bodies designed and certainly enhanced Southdown Motor Services' tours programme in 1961 when 40 on Leyland Leopard chassis were delivered with cream roofs and spacious seating. Car 1729 (2729 CD) is seen towards the end of its life at Seven Sisters Country Park, near Seaford, on a school private hire in the early 'Seventies. *John Bishop*

CONTENTS

Narrative by Glyn Kraemer-Johnson

Photographs selected and captioned by John Bishop

First published 2001

ISBN 0 7110 2793 5

All rights reserved. No part of this book may be reproduced or transmitted in any form or by any means, electronic or mechanical, including photocopying, recording or by any information storage and retrieval system, without permission from the Publisher in writing.

© Ian Allan Publishing Ltd 2001

Published by Ian Allan Publishing

an imprint of Ian Allan Publishing Ltd, Hersham, Surrey KT12 4RG.

Printed by Ian Allan Printing Ltd, Hersham, Surrey KT12 4RG.

Code: 0106/B2

Title page:
A small batch of Leyland PS2 chassis comprised six with attractive Windover bodywork. The then new Chichester bus station is the setting for this 1950s view of 1273 (HUF 273). The driver is inside the saloon, making sure the passengers are comfortable before setting off for Hindhead, Surrey, via the superb scenery of West Sussex. *Glyn Kraemer-Johnson collection*

INTRODUCTION

'Dear old Sussex by the sea…'. Beachy Head, the Royal Pavilion, Arundel Castle, Battle Abbey, Chichester Cathedral. All well-known landmarks in this lovely county, and all at one time served by the smart apple green and cream buses of Southdown Motor Services Ltd.

Both John Bishop and I were raised in Brighton — heart of Southdown territory — and grew up with a love of the Company. Prior to the Brighton Area agreement of 1961, Southdown charged protective fares throughout Brighton and Hove. This meant that higher fares were charged to deter short-distance passengers from using Southdown buses, thus protecting the local operators, Brighton, Hove & District and Brighton Corporation. For many years in my young mind I thought that one paid higher fares for the privilege of travelling on a more luxurious vehicle! And luxurious they were, with their shaped, higher-backed seats covered front and back in moquette of varying shades of brown and orange. What was more, Southdown buses had heaters, great circular chrome affairs fixed to the front bulkhead. Heaters were unknown to BH&D and the Corporation, and would remain so until the 'Sixties.

Southdown will be remembered for many things. It led the field in British and Continental coach tours — or 'Cruises', as it preferred to call them — with an immaculately-turned-out fleet of coaches, or 'cars', as Southdown vehicles were always known.

◄ No book on Southdown in its glory days would be complete without a view of a lower-deck interior — in this case that of TD3 No 969. The base colour of the interior was brown, giving a warm feeling, while Clayton Dewandre provided the practical warmth from the heater matrix. Polished dark wood added that final touch of class. *A. Bell / Glyn Kraemer-Johnson collection.*

Then there was the network of express services radiating from London to the coastal towns of Sussex and east Hampshire. To some these may evoke memories of elegant ECW-bodied Leyland PS1s, while others will remember the rasping exhausts of the Beadle-Commer integrals.

These are just a few of the things which spring to mind when the name of Southdown is mentioned, and that is what this book is all about. It is not intended to be a comprehensive history; that has already been done. Although it takes a fairly in-depth look at the vehicles operated, it does not go into a great deal of technical detail. This volume is a collection of memories of an operator that was amongst the élite of bus companies, and the authors hope it will appeal to the layman as well as the enthusiast.

Southdown's 'Glory Days' were, in the authors' opinion, the 'Thirties, 'Forties, 'Fifties and 'Sixties. The book therefore concentrates on the period from 1929, when the first Leyland Titan arrived, to 1970, by which time Southdown was under the control of the National Bus Company. Having obliterated the famous apple green and cream beneath a sea of leaf green, NBC reduced the Company to a shadow of its former self before selling it to its management; the latter then 'cashed in' by selling out to Stagecoach, under whose auspices the Southdown name ultimately disappeared altogether.

Suffice to say that Southdown Motor Services Ltd was formed in 1915 from three major operators: Worthing Motor Services, the London & South Coast Haulage Co and the country services of the Brighton, Hove & Preston United Omnibus Co.

Although during the following years a handful of smaller operators was acquired, expansion was largely due to the introduction and development of new services. However, in 1925 the business of Southsea Tourist Co Ltd of Portsmouth and Horndean was acquired, together with 30 vehicles, thus giving Southdown a foothold in east Hampshire. This was followed in 1932 by the purchase of Chapman & Son of Eastbourne, which brought with it a number of long-distance coach cruises that set Southdown on the road to becoming one of the major operators of this type of holiday, the number of tours rising from 10 in 1925 to 390 in 1951.

The acquisition of smaller companies, together with the effects of World War 2, brought a motley collection of vehicles into the fleet, but, even from the early days, Southdown showed a preference for buses of Leyland manufacture — a preference which was to last until the advent of the National Bus Company. Originally, vehicles of Dennis and particularly Tilling-Stevens

manufacture had also been bought in quite large numbers. From 1915 the British Automobile Traction Co (BAT) had had an interest in Southdown, which thus became a part of the Tilling-BAT group in 1928. In the reorganisation of 1942, Southdown came under the control of the British Electric Traction group. BET's purchasing policy had some effect on the choice and style of vehicles bought, but by no means to the same degree as with other companies within the group.

The Southdown area eventually extended from Fareham in the west to Hastings in the east, and inland as far as Petersfield, Midhurst, Horsham and East Grinstead. Its operating territory was divided into five areas: Portsmouth, Chichester/Bognor Regis, Worthing, Brighton and Eastbourne. The Head Office was situated at 5 Steine Street, Brighton, which was also home to Brighton's express coach station.

A garage had been built at Freshfield Road, Brighton, in 1916 in which were housed the Company's workshops. By 1928, however, these were proving grossly inadequate, and a new Central Works was constructed at Victoria Road, Portslade. Garages were opened in most of the major towns, with dormitory or 'dormy' sheds in the larger and sometimes not-so-large villages. The garages were equipped with maintenance facilities whilst the dormy sheds, as their name suggested, merely provided overnight accommodation, in some cases for just a single vehicle. These buildings sometimes affected services more than one might imagine. For instance, some enthusiasts have recently been puzzled by photographs of a lowbridge double-decker working in the Eastbourne area on routes that encountered no low bridges. The answer is that the dormy shed at Upper Dicker was not high enough to take a highbridge vehicle, hence the restriction.

In the 1950s Southdown opened new modern bus stations at Chichester, Bognor Regis, Lewes and Haywards Heath, those at Chichester and Lewes remaining today.

In 1946 a joint operating agreement was introduced in Portsmouth between Southdown and the City of Portsmouth Passenger Transport Department whereby services were co-ordinated and receipts pooled. It was not until 1961 that a similar agreement was put into effect in the Brighton area, doing away at last with those protective fares.

This, then, is the backcloth against which this book is set.

Glyn Kraemer-Johnson
Hailsham, East Sussex
February 2001

◀◀ By the time of this photograph, just over a decade had passed since Southdown Motor Services came into being. Already, the garage at Freshfield Road, Brighton, had outlived its usefulness as the Company's overhaul works, and Victoria Road, Portslade, had thus been commissioned. Second-hand Daimler Y No 17 (CD 5217) stands forlorn, with nobody looking at the 'standard' 1920s Leyland G7, by now having had its solid tyres replaced with pneumatics. Spare seats are stacked with a sewing machine in front. To the right is a Model T Ford being cared for by the Company.
courtesy Branch (2) Brighton

1. THE TD ERA

The introduction of the Leyland Titan TD1 in 1927 was probably one of the most important landmarks in the development of the motor bus. It certainly set the basic design for the double-decker until the advent of the rear-engined chassis. It had several notable features including a six-cylinder 6.8-litre engine, vacuum brakes and, most importantly, a low frame-height. This did away with the multi-step entrances of earlier types, and also allowed for a covered top to be fitted within the permitted maximum height.

Another innovation which was to last for a further 20-odd years was the production of a low-height or 'lowbridge' version of Leyland's own body allowing a laden overall height of 12ft 10in. This was achieved by fitting bench seats for four on the nearside of the upper deck, with a sunken gangway on the offside, which protruded into the lower saloon. It was a cumbersome arrangement, particularly for fare collection, and countless passengers sitting on the offside of the lower deck cracked their skulls on the sunken gangway when leaving their seat. However, the advantages outweighed the disadvantages and increased the popularity of the double-decker, especially in rural areas.

The Leyland-bodied TD1 with enclosed staircase was not that different from rear-entrance buses built in the 1960s, and would probably not turn too many heads if seen on the roads today. It was strange, therefore, that when Southdown purchased its first TD1s, numbered 801-23 (UF 4801-23), it chose to fit them with open-top, open-staircase bodies by Brush, to a somewhat antiquated design. As well as the open top and staircase, the upper deck did not extend over the driver's cab, and the windows on the 5½-bay body extended upwards to the waistband, with inward-opening vents above the main windows — obviously a throwback to tramcar design. They were quite long-lived, however, and during World War 2 were all fitted with green canvas top-covers that clearly offered passengers greater protection but resulted in some very weird-looking buses.

In 1936 Brighton, Hove & District fitted 10 of its AEC Regents with new open-top bodies for what was to become the famous open-top Sea Front Service from Portslade to Rottingdean. This set a trend for open-top services in coastal resorts; Southdown took up the idea with its service 27 from Brighton to Devil's Dyke, and other services followed. However, instead of rebodying or converting existing vehicles, Southdown simply used its Brush-bodied TD1s.

At first sight, the bodies on Southdown's second batch of TD1s were a strange choice, for they carried Leyland bodies of lowbridge layout — strange because Southdown had few low bridges in its area, but lowbridge bodies were chosen on the assumption that they would suffer less damage from overhanging trees. In all, 54 Leyland-bodied TD1s were delivered in 1929/30, these taking fleetnumbers 824-77 (with various UF 5xxx and 6xxx registrations). The last 12 were of highbridge layout, and all had enclosed staircases. The covered-top double-deckers introduced a slightly modified livery to the fleet. The apple green and cream was retained, but now the beading above and below the windows was lined out in dark green with, on the lower deck, a thin gold line beneath the dark green.

In 1931 two further batches of TD1s arrived — Nos 878-81 (UF 7078-81) and 882-932 (UF 7382-7432) — which carried highbridge bodies by Short Bros. The outward appearance of these was not that dissimilar to the Leyland body, the most noticeable differences being a much deeper roof, shallower windows and 'V'-shaped windows at the front of the upper deck. 1932/3 orders called for the new Leyland TD2, an updated version of the TD1 fitted with the larger 7.6-litre petrol engine. Again, Short Bros bodies were specified, seating 50, and these vehicles materialised as Nos 933-59 (UF 8373-83, 8844-54, 9755-9).

It seemed that every year saw the introduction of a new double-deck chassis design from Leyland, and 1933 was no exception, with the introduction of the TD3. On this chassis, the engine and radiator had been moved forward, giving more room for increased seating capacity on the lower deck. A new and more modern-looking radiator was also

◄ This view of highbridge all-Leyland Titan TD1 868 (UF 6468) dating from 1930 demonstrates the strides already taken in double-deck bus design; the 'piano' front would feature for a number of years. The lining-out enhances the design, while the familiar Clark's Bread advertisement adorned many Brighton and Worthing buses of the day. *courtesy of the Omnibus Society*

◄ By 1932 Short Bros had cornered the market in Southdown's orders, and was thus chosen to body Leyland Titan TD2 935 (UF 8375). The style of front combined with six-bay construction was the design of the day. The route number was on side slip-boards with adequate information emphasised on the destination screen. 'SOUTHDOWN' is proudly emblazoned on the front below the destination. *courtesy of the Omnibus Society*

fitted. Southdown took 16 of the new chassis in
1934, numbering them 960-75 (AUF 660-75). Short
Bros again supplied the bodywork, which was to a
more modern and pleasing design. The 'V'-shaped
front upper-deck windows had gone, and there was
a gentle slope to the front profile. In spite of the
modifications to the chassis and increased space at
the front of the lower deck, Southdown, always
putting passenger comfort first, again specified a
seating capacity of just 50.

The first four of the batch were classified 'TD3c'
and were what was known as 'Gearless Buses', being
fitted with torque converters. The torque converter
was an early attempt at a fully-automatic gearbox.
The 'gear lever' had four positions: direct, converter,
neutral and reverse — there was no clutch pedal.
'Converter' mode was normally selected from rest
until the vehicle reached about 20mph, when 'direct'
would be engaged. Starting from rest, the engine
speed would rise rapidly to about 1,200rpm. 'Direct'
would then be selected, and the engine speed would
remain constant in spite of the increasing or
decreasing speed of the vehicle. The system was not entirely
successful, and most operators who had specified converters
(including London Transport, with its love of preselector
gearboxes) removed them at some stage of the vehicles' lives.
Southdown was no exception, and 960-3 were converted to
normal gearboxes when fitted with oil engines.

Eight of the remaining TD3s marked another major
milestone in the development of the Southdown bus, being
fitted with diesel engines from new. The engine was the
famous Leyland 8.6-litre unit, which was to continue in
production until after World War 2. Another feature of these
buses was that all were originally fitted with folding sunshine
roofs, although these, too, were subsequently removed.

Unlike many companies that continued to use boards, all
Southdown Titans had been fitted with roller-blind destination
equipment, at the front on early models, and the rear as well
on enclosed-staircase vehicles. As Southdown's operating
territory was one frequently visited by holidaymakers and
day-trippers, good route information was essential and
Southdown rose to the challenge. Initially, additional
information had been given on boards fitted below the lower-
deck windows. However, the TD3s included roller-blind

destination screens above the lower-deck windows. These consisted of three screens, showing ultimate destination, route number and 'via' points. At first they were fitted to the nearside only, but later vehicles featured them on the offside as well. A side-effect of these screens was the rather odd appearance given to the inside of the lower saloon, the cove panels of which featured an array of peepholes and handles enabling the conductor to change the blinds from inside the vehicle.

The TD3s set the pattern for the rest of the decade. TD4s were purchased in 1935/6 (fleetnumbers recommencing at 100), and TD5s from 1937 to 1939, but they differed little from the TD3. The diesel engine became standard, and the throaty roar of the 8.6-litre engine

1936 saw a break with Short Bros and the start of a long affair with Beadle, which built the lowbridge body on Titan TD4 No 140 (CCD 940). The fashions and the Austin car give a distinctive early-postwar feel to this view. Note the lack of lining-out, and the (dark green) painted radiator. *W. J. Haynes / Southdown Enthusiasts' Club*

became a familiar sound throughout the area. Short Bros bodied the 1935 intake, but from then until 1939 bodywork orders were split between Beadle and Park Royal, both of which produced basically similar-looking bodies featuring outswept skirt panels and six-bay construction. Both companies supplied bodies of highbridge and lowbridge layout to an increased seating capacity of 52. The height of the body was distinguished by the fleetnumber, which had either an 'H' or an 'L' suffix.

By 1939 and the outbreak of war, Southdown was operating some 340 Leyland TD double-deckers. A further 27 were on order for delivery in 1940, these being of the latest TD7 type, which featured flexible engine mountings. Bodies were by Park Royal, incorporating a smooth frontal profile with no protrusions. Twenty-three were of highbridge layout, the remaining four being lowbridge. They were to have been numbered 266-92, and received Brighton registrations GCD 666-92. However, Southdown's operating territory, stretching as it did along the Sussex and Hampshire coast, would have been in the front line should the threat of invasion have been realised. The Ministry of War therefore imposed restrictions on travel in the area and, of course, holidaymakers and day-trippers disappeared overnight. It was thought that these factors would drastically reduce traffic, and the TD7s were therefore diverted to other operators, 16 going to Crosville, seven to Western Welsh and the four lowbridge buses to Cumberland.

Wilts & Dorset Motor Services was very closely associated with Southdown, even to the extent that for many years its affairs had been run from Southdown's Worthing office. Vehicle specification and livery, albeit red, were pure Southdown. (Take a look at a black and white photograph of a prewar Wilts & Dorset coach and the point will be proven.) Following the outbreak of war the military greatly increased its activities on Salisbury Plain, with a consequent growth in transport requirements. Wilts & Dorset found itself unable to cope with the increase and Southdown came to the rescue. No fewer than 41 TD1s, together with 17 other buses, were transferred to the Salisbury-based fleet. Through the loss of these vehicles and the fact that the Government appeared to have overlooked the additional traffic created by increased activity at Portsmouth Dockyard, Southdown found that it too was suffering a vehicle shortage, and had to hire in vehicles — all TDs — from East Kent and Eastbourne Corporation.

Mention has already been made of the 23 open-top TD1s, all of which received green canvas top-covers in 1941. Only eight of the closed-top TD1s remained, and it was decided in 1943 that these, together with 13 TD2s, should be rebodied and the chassis reconditioned. By this stage of the war, the Ministry of Supply had introduced its utility specification for bus bodies. Basically this meant replacing all curved surfaces with flat panels, resulting in an angular and not very attractive design. In practice,

◄◄ For the war years the Brush open-top bodies were given canvas roofs, exemplified by this view of 807 (UF 4807). Note, under the fleetnumber, the letter 'H' to signify this is a highbridge vehicle. The barbed wire in the background gives a good indication of the war effort to keep the enemy out. *courtesy of the Omnibus Society*

◄ This fascinating photograph taken inside Portslade Works in 1951 catches Northern Counties-bodied Guy Arab 401 (GCD 975) alongside rebodied TD2 Leyland 956 (UF 9756) with its East Lancs body which will be surrendered to 401. The shine on 401 is surprising, considering it was about to be rebodied, but nevertheless shows the standard set by Southdown. *courtesy of the Omnibus Society*

however, bodybuilders tended to apply their own interpretation of the specification, resulting in some widely differing degrees of austerity.

Two bodybuilders had been selected by the Ministry of Supply to build on reconditioned chassis, namely East Lancashire Coachbuilders and Willowbrook. Park Royal was also chosen by Southdown to carry out some of the rebodying. Willowbrook produced one of the most angular and unattractive of all the utility bodies and was chosen to produce lowbridge bodies, which did little to help the overall appearance. The highbridge bodies were built by Park Royal, which turned out an angular but not displeasing version, and East Lancs, whose design abounded in gentle curves and was not very far removed from its standard postwar product. Unlike rebodied TDs of many other operators, the Southdown buses retained their original radiators. Willowbrook was again called upon in 1944 to rebuild the bodies on four TD3 and TD4 chassis, whilst others were refurbished by Portsmouth Aviation, Beadle, Saunders and West Nor.

◄ Being shown off to full advantage at Southsea, the new Beadle six-bay body on Leyland TD5 No 153 (DUF 153) replaced the 1937 Park Royal original in 1948. This was part of a major undertaking by Southdown to rebody the prewar Titans, and the contract was shared by Beadle, Park Royal, East Lancs, Northern Counties and Saunders. *courtesy of the Omnibus Society*

Car 165 (EUF 165), a 1938 Leyland TD5 with new (1949) Park Royal highbridge body, stands resplendent in its Southdown livery at Pool Valley, Brighton, ready to depart on route 16 to Hailsham. The 16 would later be truncated to Golden Cross (between Hailsham and Uckfield), where a connection could then be made with route 92 to Eastbourne and Hailsham. *W. J. Haynes / Southdown Enthusiasts' Club*

Photographed at Pool Valley towards the end of its life, 199 (EUF 199), another TD5, shows the Saunders body. The dark green lining has gone, the stair window has been painted over, and the bus is now relegated to relief work on the main Brighton–Horsham route. *Photobus*

The later Beadle (1949/50) rebodies would be of five-bay construction, making for a cleaner, less cluttered look. TD5 No 187 (EUF 187) looks almost new in this view in Worthing. Advertisements indicate the postwar trends in smoking (Goldflake cigarettes) and drinking (Monument sherry). *Eric Surfleet / Glyn Kraemer-Johnson collection*

The back of a bus frequently has as much character as the front, yet is seldom shown. This is rectified with a rear nearside view of 213 (FCD 513), a 1939 Leyland Titan TD5 loading in Hastings *en route* for Eastbourne. The bodywork is a lowbridge Park Royal design, with wartime dark green roof. One can almost smell the Bisto in the advertisement! *courtesy of the Omnibus Society*

A more conventional view of the same bus at Pool Valley makes for an interesting comparison with the previous picture, inasmuch as 213 has by now been rebodied with a highbridge East Lancs design. It is seen with full postwar lining around the roof and horizontally along the body. This view also illustrates the aforementioned truncation of the 16 route to Golden Cross, near Hailsham. The traditional 'SOUTHDOWN' on the fascia of the travel office was exposed recently when Pool Valley was cleaned and tidied for the use of express coaches. *W. J. Haynes / Southdown Enthusiasts' Club*

13

By the time hostilities ceased in 1945, many of the TDs had reached a state where rebuilding would not be sufficient, and a major rebodying programme was embarked upon. Between 1946 and 1950 no fewer than 152 TD3s, 4s and 5s received new bodies to postwar standards. Five bodybuilders were chosen to carry out the work: East Lancs, Park Royal, Beadle, Saunders and Northern Counties. Each company built to its own standard design with little variation to suit Southdown, except perhaps for the metal sun-visor fitted above the windscreen (which was something of a Southdown trademark) and, in some cases, a semi-circular staircase window, which had been standard on prewar 'deckers. The first East Lancs bodies were 52-seaters, the remainder and those of the other coachbuilders having a capacity of 54. The Park Royal, East Lancs and Saunders bodies were all fairly similar in appearance. Beadle, for some reason, built bodies of both five- and six-bay construction, which were little different from its prewar design. The Northern Counties bodies were easily identified by the heavily-radiused corners of the front and rear windows.

The new bodies differed internally as well. While all had the standard Southdown moquette of various shades of brown and orange, the seats themselves varied between vehicles. Some had low backs with a curved top and stainless-steel grab rails, some had high, straight backs with unpolished metal rails that looked as if they might have come from the original bodies, and some had the high shaped backs which were the postwar Southdown standard. East Lancs, Saunders and Park Royal used brown and cream rexine on the window pillars. Beadle stuck to varnished wood, whilst, if memories can be trusted, Northern Counties painted its pillars a strange khaki colour.

Although rarely used on the premier services such as the 12 (Brighton–Eastbourne) and 31 (Brighton–Southsea), the TDs were the mainstay of the inland routes for many years. Apart from those huge round Clayton Dewandre heaters, the most lasting impression of the TDs is of the sound effects — that deep-throated roar as they pulled away in second gear, changing to a higher-pitched and much quieter sound when third was engaged.

With the influx of new vehicles throughout the 'Fifties, the numbers of TDs began to dwindle. The last was withdrawn in 1962, by which time some had completed 25 years' service. Thus the unmistakable roar of the prewar Leyland diesel gave way to the genteel tickover of the PD2 and the raucous exhaust of the PD3.

2. THE LEYLAND ZOO: TIGERS, LIONESSES, CHEETAHS AND CUBS

As 1930 had seen the change from open-top, open-staircase double-deckers to something approaching the bus we know today, so the same year saw changes almost as dramatic to the coach and single-decker.

At the dawning of the new decade, Southdown was firmly wedded to the Tilling-Stevens for its single-deck requirements. From 1928 to 1931 some 115 B10A2 chassis had been delivered, with bodies by either Short Bros of Rochester or Harrington of Hove, although one small batch received Tilling bodies; all seated about 30 and had rear entrances. The Tilling-Stevens 'Express', as it was known, was a considerable improvement over what had gone before, with forward control and a lower frame-height making access easier. The bodies, however, were in something of a transitional stage between Edwardian austerity and the flowing lines that were to come. They had a very upright frontal profile with a large roof-mounted destination box, the latter being to Southdown specification. As with the double-deckers, roller blinds were fitted.

In 1929/30, 69 Tilling-Stevens Express chassis were taken into stock for coaching work. These were of type B10B2, being normal-control with a distinctive sloping bonnet. Most were given bodies by Harrington, to various designs, while one batch was bodied by Short Bros and some received Harrington charabanc bodies from earlier vehicles.

One of Southdown's predecessors, Sussex Motor Road Car, had built up a network of extended coach tours, or 'cruises', as they became known, both in Great Britain and on the Continent, together with excursions to race meetings and the like. Unfortunately, World War 1 put an abrupt stop to these activities, and after the armistice the three-year-old Southdown company was too busy trying to restore and re-equip its stage-carriage services to worry about such things.

The restoration of coach tours got off to a very slow start, and it was not until 1931, when Southdown took over the business of Chapman of Eastbourne together with 50 vehicles, that the coach cruise once again became firmly established. Before long, however, these covered the length and breadth of Britain. Southdown took no short-cuts when it came to coach cruises,

stopping at only the best hotels. Indeed, it became a sign of prestige for an hotelier to have a Southdown coach parked outside his premises. Only the *crème de la crème* of drivers was chosen for touring work, and, needless to say, the vehicles used were to the same high standard.

Day and half-day excursions were also reintroduced from the major seaside towns. Right up until the 'Sixties, a feature of a walk along the prom at Eastbourne, Brighton or Worthing was a line of gleaming Southdown coaches, each with a blackboard leaning against the wheel or the beading (never the paintwork), advertising the tour to be taken. These boards were almost works of art, being beautifully written and in some cases illustrated in coloured chalks. Looking at them was almost like visiting an art gallery. Drivers of coaches from some of the smaller operators would accost passers-by in an attempt to increase trade, but Southdown drivers rarely (if ever) followed suit. They were much too dignified.

The other important coaching activity was, of course, express services. These too had been gradually increasing throughout the 'Twenties, with a complete network of services from London to the major resorts in Sussex and east Hampshire. In 1932 came another major express service, this being the South Coast Express from Margate to Bournemouth, which was operated jointly with East Kent and Royal Blue. These, then, were the operations for which Southdown required coaches in 1930.

Because of the large intake of Tilling-Stevens single-deckers and coaches, it was not until 1930 that the first Leyland Tiger appeared in the fleet. The Tiger TS1, introduced in 1927, was the single-deck version of the Titan TD1, having most parts in common. It had a wheelbase of 17ft 6in and was designed to take bodywork of 27ft 6in overall length. In 1928 the TS2 was introduced. This was virtually identical to the TS1, with the same wheelbase but built to take bodywork of 26ft overall.

Southdown's first Tigers were TS2s with rather severe-looking bodies by London Lorries purchased for express services. They were 26-seaters equipped with front and rear doors, and began a new number series starting at 1001. The first Harrington-bodied examples, also delivered in 1930, were to the same configuration, but on the 1931 intake the front door was eliminated and the seating capacity increased to 30. Harrington really went to town on the TS2 chassis, producing an elegant body that was to set the pattern for the rest of the decade. Not only was the exterior quite handsome, but additionally the interior offered a high standard of comfort with curtains at the windows, plush seating and polished woodwork. A third body-builder was contracted to build for the TS2 and this was a firm called Hoyal, about which little seems to be known. Hoyal bodied the last five Tigers to be delivered in 1931, these being Southdown's first TS1s to the longer overall length of 27ft 6in.

The Tilling-Stevens Express and Leyland Tiger had brought the forward-control (ie with the driver beside the engine) chassis into the fleet for stage-carriage and express work but, for its extended tours, Southdown continued to specify normal-control (bonneted) chassis. Thus in 1930 came 11 Leyland Lioness coaches, to be followed by a further six in 1933. The Lioness, introduced as early as 1925, was the normal-control version of the Lion, the latter being a Leyland model that never found its way into the Southdown fleet. Although basically similar to its male counterpart, the Lioness had a smaller engine of only 3.96-litre capacity, which seems minute by today's standards but which appears to have been man enough for the job. Harrington built the bodies on all 17, and its designers really took up the challenge to produce what turned out to be something like a huge luxurious limousine. Only 20 plush seats were fitted in the rear-entrance bodies, which had the usual folding canvas roof. In later life they were rebuilt with centre entrances and a fixed roof with glass cant panels and a folding centre section. In this form they remained in service on coach cruises until as late as 1952, by which time they looked extremely dated but were still luxurious by any standard.

Although the emphasis was now firmly on Leyland products, Southdown did purchase three Tilling-Stevens — or TSM, as that

THUN.

company was now known — chassis to its C60A7 specification in 1931. They were given Harrington bodies virtually identical to those on the TS2s and were put to work on express services. They were not, however, the last TSMs to enter the fleet. In 1932 six B9B chassis were bought from Thames Valley and given Park Royal coach bodies taken from vehicles acquired with the business of Chapman of Eastbourne.

The smaller operators and their vehicles which were taken over by Southdown at this time are far too numerous and varied to mention. One that does warrant inclusion, however, is Chapman & Sons of Eastbourne, which passed to Southdown in March 1932. With this business came not only express services to London but a network of British and Continental tours. Chapman had fitted pneumatic tyres to his fleet of Dennis charabancs back in the 'Twenties and had subsequently built up a healthy reputation in this field. Some 50 vehicles, mainly of Maudslay and Dennis manufacture, were taken over with the Chapman business, although also included were two formidable-looking Lancia Pentiota normal-control coaches.

Six new TSM B39A6 chassis were received in 1933 to work on the Hayling Island service. Langstone Bridge, which connected Hayling Island with the mainland, had severe weight restrictions that were to limit the type of vehicle used on this service for many years to come. Accordingly the TSMs were fitted with all-metal lightweight bodies built by Short Bros. All six were commandeered by the War Department in 1940.

Also commandeered were 24 Leyland Tiger TS4s delivered to Southdown in 1932/3. The TS4 was built to take bodywork of 27ft 6in overall length and had a 7.6-litre engine. There were other refinements over previous Tigers. Bodies were again by Harrington to the same basic pattern as those fitted to the TS2s. Some of those commandeered were returned after the war and lasted until the mid-'Fifties. One of these coaches was fitted with a full-length roof luggage rack and was used exclusively for transporting the Band of the Royal Marines, Portsmouth.

Another Leyland model new to Southdown was the Cub, two of which were received in 1933. The Cub had a 4.4-litre petrol engine and was available as normal- or forward-control and with several wheelbases. Southdown's pair were of type KP2, with a 14ft wheelbase that would accommodate bodies with a seating capacity of 20. They were to normal-control design and had Harrington bodies with folding canvas roofs and, being intended for the shorter coach tours, seats for just 14, although they were up-seated to 20 in 1949.

Since the end of World War 1, Southdown vehicles had been registered in Brighton, receiving that authority's CD or UF registration letters. The Cubs, given fleetnumbers 1 and 2, introduced the three-letter marks to the fleet, being registered ACD 101/2.

Southdown's next new purchases were three Leyland Tiger TS6s, which arrived in 1934 and, in line with the TD3 double-decker, featured a revised front end and radiator. Harrington built the 32-seat rear-entrance bodies, which still carried a roof-mounted luggage rack but to a more aerodynamic design, and the interior saw new standards of comfort.

Also in 1934 came two very interesting vehicles, numbered 50/1 (AUF 850/1). These were Leyland TS6Ts, which were six-wheel 30ft single-deckers with twin axles at the rear. At the time, four-wheel vehicles were not permitted to exceed 26ft in length. The extra length was required because the Traffic Commissioners would not allow double-deckers to operate on the Eastbourne to Beachy Head service, and the longer buses could accommodate 40 passengers compared with 32 in a normal single-decker. Short Bros built the centre-entrance bodies, producing a design that was rather more severe than the Harrington version which was to appear later, although it was intended to look as much as

possible like the contemporary coach bodies, even to the roof route boards. The extra length gave the buses a massive appearance, particularly inside.

From 1935 to 1937 some 120 Leyland TS7s were taken into stock, the TS7 being the single-deck version of the Titan TD4. Ninety of these chassis received coach bodies by a variety of manufacturers including Harrington, Beadle, Park Royal and, for the first time, H. V. Burlingham of Blackpool. All were rear-entrance 32-seaters. Although all were to the same basic design, the Burlingham bodies featured a wider waistband which gave them a more bus-like appearance.

No 1083 (UF 9783), a 1933 Leyland Tiger TS4 with 32-seat Harrington coachwork, is seen on Eastbourne's seafront on route 97 to the Top of Beachy Head. To this day the layout of the road at this point makes it necessary to pull up away from the kerbside, as depicted. Vehicles apart, this location is little changed today. *courtesy of the Omnibus Society*

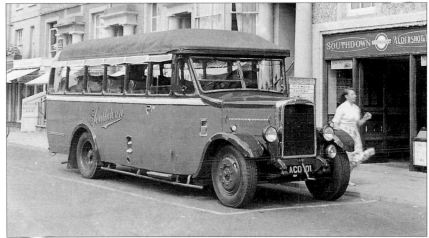

The Carfax, Horsham, is the setting for this view of 1 (ACD 101), a Leyland Cub with Harrington coachwork. No 1 was delivered with 14 seats for tour work, but in 1949 was upseated to accommodate 20 passengers. This was a time when any town of reasonable size had a travel office to deal with enquiries and handle parcels. Three operators — Southdown Motor Services, Aldershot & District Traction Co and London Transport, all of which had a strong presence in Horsham — shared this office. *V. C. Jones / Southdown Enthusiasts' Club*

No 50 (AUF 850) was one of a brace of three-axle Leyland Tiger TS6Ts with Short Bros bodies delivered in 1934 especially for the Beachy Head route from Eastbourne; it was decreed at the time that the route was unsuitable for double-deck vehicles. The rear wheels were in fact trailing and not driven from the engine. *courtesy of the Omnibus Society*

Car 1135 (CCD 735) was a Beadle-bodied Leyland Tiger TS7 delivered in 1936. This view shows very clearly the 'Southdown' badge where 'Leyland' would normally be on the radiator; this was to remain a feature until NBC days. Dicker Pottery, situated near Hailsham, has long since gone. Almost incredibly, the quiet road featured here is in fact the main Eastbourne–London A22! *courtesy of the Omnibus Society*

Seen passing Hilsea garage on the outskirts of Portsmouth, 1152 (CUF 152) was a Leyland Tiger TS7 with Burlingham body, the latter's rounded edges giving it an elegance befitting the Southdown name. In the distance is a Portsmouth Corporation Leyland Titan. *Southdown Enthusiasts' Club.*

The remaining TS7s received bus bodies by Harrington and started a new numbering sequence from 1400. They were to a new design especially for (and unique to) Southdown, and were to become classics of their time. No doubt if the preservation movement had been active at the time of their withdrawal, preserved examples would be as numerous as 'Queen Mary' Leyland PD3s. Alas, none has survived. Some basically similar vehicles were delivered to Maidstone & District, registered in the FKO series, but these lacked the many refinements specified by Southdown.

The bodies of the '1400s', as they became known, featured curved glass quarter panels at the rear, which gave passengers 'all-round' visibility, although they were panelled over on rebuild after World War 2. They also featured three-aperture destination screens on each side above the windows, the same as fitted to contemporary double-deckers. In addition there were large screens at front and rear. In retrospect it was strange that Southdown went to so much trouble to provide a generous destination display when vehicles were frequently seen displaying the single unhelpful word 'Relief' with no indication as to the route being operated. Internally, they were finished to a very high standard, such that they could be used on coaching work if required. Seats were high-backed and introduced the brown, orange and fawn moquette to the single-decker. They were finished in a striking livery of apple green with cream roof and waistband. During the war the cream roofs were repainted dark green to make them less conspicuous from the air, and this subsequently became the standard postwar single-deck livery.

More '1400s' were delivered in 1938/9, bringing the total number in stock to 86. These were mounted on the revised TS8 chassis, which differed only in detail from its predecessor.

These handsome little buses formed the backbone of the single-deck fleet throughout the war, being supplemented by the few coaches that had not been requisitioned. During the war most of the '1400s' received new perimeter seating around the sides of the saloon, leaving a space in the middle for standees. This increased their capacity to 60, a figure that was frequently needed. One can only try to imagine the conductor's task of collecting fares in a bus full of standing passengers. As if this wasn't enough in itself, at each terminus he — or more probably she — would have to change at least four destination blinds. If the service ran through one of the larger towns he/she would also be required to report to the local bus office, giving details of the names of the conductor and driver, the number of passengers

carried and the fleet number of the bus. In addition, the waybill would have to be completed at the end of each journey to give details of tickets sold.

It was a credit both to Southdown and to Leyland Motors that these single-deckers were kept in service day after day throughout the dark years of the war when both labour and materials were in short supply. Running repairs were sometimes necessary, and on one occasion a '1400' arrived in Hailsham with a flat tyre. After a lengthy wait, a fitter appeared with a spare wheel strapped to the roof of a Morris 8 car. The change was made in Hailsham High Street, and the bus went on its way an hour and a half late. Unfortunately one of this class, 1443, did not survive the war unscathed. On 2 November 1940 it was attacked by enemy aircraft and was blown down an embankment in Punnett's Town (near Heathfield), killing five passengers. The bus received a new Harrington coach body in May 1941 and survived in this form until 1952.

In 1945 those buses which had received perimeter seating reverted to their original layout. Many were rebuilt by a variety of firms not usually associated with bus bodybuilding, such as Caffyns, Portsmouth Aviation, Lancashire Aircraft, Aircraft Dispatch and Southdown itself. In rebuilt condition they

▲ Perhaps it is arguable, but in my view this must qualify as the all-time classic single-decker, a locally-built Harrington body mounted on a Leyland Tiger TS chassis. Car 1407 (BUF 987), a 1935 TS7, is seen on Worthing seafront, with a Leyland PD2 in the distance. The 'Autovac' to bring the fuel up from the tank to the engine is visible below the front nearside screen.
W. J. Haynes / Southdown Enthusiasts' Club

▲ This view of Leyland TS7/Harrington 1424 (DCD 324), at Rottingdean on the 12B bound for Brighton railway station, exudes atmosphere. The now busy coast road is completely traffic-free, while parked on the landward side is a prewar Ford Model Y. *Geoff Maynard collection*

▲ No 1428 (DCD 328) does not look so grand in this view, with its side destination screens painted over, while a paper 'Relief' destination display does little to enhance this classic vehicle at Pool Valley, Brighton. The lowbridge TD5/Beadle alongside, 188 (EUF 188), which always retained this body, looks down on 1428 as if in superior manner! *W. J. Haynes / Southdown Enthusiasts' Club*

▼ No 1469 (FCD 369) represents the 1938/9 intake of TS8 Tigers. It is seen literally grinding up over High and Over, between Alfriston and Seaford, on route 126. This was a long inland route from Eastbourne to Seaford, as opposed to the direct, coastal route followed by the 12, which continued to Brighton. *courtesy of the Omnibus Society*

▼ Our views of the '1400' class conclude with this shot of 1463 (FCD 263). Seen at Haywards Heath, it has full, informative rear destination blind; note also the 'stopping' sign on the offside rear. A deep score by the fleetname mars the side of the vehicle. *Glyn Kraemer-Johnson collection*

soldiered on into the early to mid-'Fifties, when they were replaced by new Leyland Royal Tigers and Tiger Cubs. Even then their working days were not strictly over, for many of them donated running units to be used in the Beadle rebuilds which utilised prewar running units in a postwar integral body, described later on in this volume. Ironically 1443 was one such donor, its parts going to build 876 (later renumbered 653) and in this form remaining in service until 1965. Even the Luftwaffe couldn't keep down a good '1400'!

1935 had also seen the arrival of 52/3 (BUF 552/3), two more six-wheelers needed to cope with extra traffic on the Beachy Head service. Based on the revised TS7 chassis, they were classified TS7T. Again, they had 40-seat centre entrance bodies by Short Bros. For obvious reasons the 97 service to Beachy Head was withdrawn during the war years and all four six-wheelers were transferred to Brighton; they were put to work on service 30 (Brighton–Chelwood Common) and, during their layover at Brighton, local service 13F to Lower Bevendean. Surprising (but typical of Southdown) was the fact that they continued to carry roof-boards freshly painted for services 30 and 13F. After the war they returned to their original haunt until 1952, when the Traffic Commissioners finally sanctioned the use of double-deckers to the Top of Beachy Head and the six-wheel Tigers were replaced by open-top double-deckers.

Six rather special coaches were delivered in 1936. They were based on the Leyland Tigress chassis, this being an updated version of the Lioness. Nos 318-23 (CUF 318-23) were normal-control bonneted models and were fitted with 32-seat bodies by Burlingham. The interior specification was particularly lavish, with a two-plus-one seating arrangement, the seats themselves being plush armchairs. They had glass cant panels and curved glass quarterlights at the rear, which together gave passengers an excellent all-round view, ideal for the long-distance coach tours for which they were

In 1935 two more three-axle, Short Bros-bodied Tigers were delivered for the ever-increasing trade to Beachy Head. These were TS7Ts; 53 (BUF 553) is seen on Eastbourne seafront, complete with side destination boards. *Geoff Rixon*

Car 323 (CUF 323) was a Burlingham-bodied Leyland Tigress. She stands outside Victoria Road Works, Portslade, with general trade plates 471 AP. At this period there were also limited trade plates which had very stringent rules rigorously enforced by the Police, and were therefore not very popular with fleet operators. No 323 was one of six, delivered for tour work, which were the last word in luxury. *Eric Surfleet /Glyn Kraemer-Johnson collection*

The Harrington coachwork on the Leyland Cub was full of elegance, apparent from this view of 1937-built 34 (CCD 704). At the time, Southdown was not shy to place its name on the destination screen, which would be illuminated at night. *W. J. Haynes / Southdown Enthusiasts' Club*

intended. They remained on these tours until well after the war, finally being withdrawn in 1952.

The years 1936-9 saw the continued arrival of coaches and single-deckers much as before. Twenty-seat Cubs were delivered with either Harrington coach bodies or rather austere-looking bus bodies by Park Royal, the latter being very similar to London Transport's C-class Leyland Cubs. Three of the Harrington-bodied examples, Nos 3-5, were of only 21ft 8in overall length and had a seating capacity of just 14. More Tigers were received too, some having Harrington bus bodies as already described, the remainder being fitted with 32-seat coach bodies by either Harrington or Park Royal.

No 25 (ECD 525) was a 1937 Park Royal-bodied Leyland Cub, seen on private-hire work at Haywards Heath railway station. The Park Royal design always had a very functional appearance in bus form. *W. J. Haynes / Southdown Enthusiasts' Club*

This view shows how the individuality of Southdown Motor Services extended to its garages. No 20 (ECD 520) is seen in front of Dane Road garage, Seaford. *Glyn Kraemer-Johnson collection*

Victoria Coach Station is the setting for 506 (FUF 506), a 1939 Park Royal-bodied Leyland Cheetah purchased by virtue of its lighter weight for use on Hayling Island. The 1950s were the halcyon years on Hayling Island, where all the odd smaller vehicles could be seen. How grand these vehicles looked with 'SOUTHDOWN' proudly displayed over the destination screen. *D. A. Jones / London Trolleybus Preservation Society*

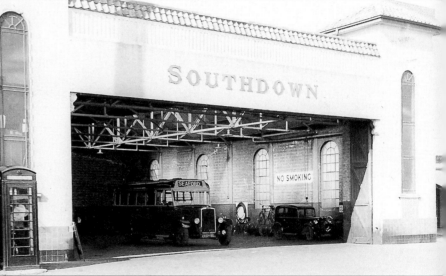

Another type to join the fleet for the first time was the Leyland Cheetah, five of which arrived in 1938 and a further six in 1939. These were given coach bodies by Park Royal, the resulting vehicle being much lighter than the Tiger. The 11 vehicles, numbered 500-10 (EUF 500-4, FUF 505-10), spent their entire lives working express services and excursions in the Havant/Hayling Island area, where their light weight was once again necessary in negotiating the notorious Langstone Bridge. They were withdrawn as soon as the bridge was replaced by a more substantial structure in 1956.

3. AT WAR WITH THE ARABS

Building chassis to a rigid and very basic specification from heavyweight metals, which were subsequently fitted with unattractive bodies built from poor-quality materials, would hardly seem to be the best way of attracting new customers, but that was what happened with Guy. Indeed, impressed by the reliability and economy of the wartime Arab, many operators were to come back for more after the cessation of hostilities, and Southdown would be no exception.

For the first four years of my life, which coincided with the last four years of the war, I lived in north Kent in an area served exclusively by London Transport's Country Area, and therefore never came face to face with a utility bus until 1946, when the family moved to Hove. I soon became familiar with Brighton, Hove & District's utility Bristol K6As and its two Guy Arabs with Pickering bodies, but it was not until 1947 that I came into contact with Southdown's examples. In that year we had a school outing to Hassocks. Everyone was ecstatic at the thought of a day away from the classroom on what was the first outing since before the war, but their excitement was nothing compared to mine when I saw the vehicle provided for the trip, one of Southdown's utility Guys with lowbridge body. Sixty shouting schoolboys made it difficult to appreciate the cacophony of sound emanating from the engine and gearbox, but the upper-deck seats for four and sunken side gangway were certainly a novelty.

The sound effects were, not unnaturally, much the same as those emitted by the BH&D Guys, and were a joy to the ears. As well as the familiar knocking of the Gardner 5LW there was a metallic, almost bell-like clatter, and above it all a high-pitched whistle which rose and fell with the engine revs. Add to this the creaking of the woodwork and one was treated to a veritable symphony! The Gardner 5LW was well known for the vibrations it produced, and when installed in a vehicle fitted with slatted wooden seats those vibrations reached parts of the anatomy that other engines couldn't reach! One can only imagine what a shock these buses must have been to passengers and crews alike after the plush interiors and smooth running of the prewar Leylands.

The Guys were not, of course, Southdown's own choice. During the war Leyland was heavily engaged in building tanks

and other military vehicles. Realising that many companies were in desperate need of new vehicles, the Ministry of Supply eventually sanctioned three manufacturers, namely Bristol, Daimler and Guy, to build double-deck chassis to a rigid specification. Similarly a number of bodybuilders were selected to construct bodies, again to a firm specification which featured no curved surfaces, few opening windows and diminutive headlights. In practice, however, the resulting vehicles differed quite considerably in their degree of austerity.

Whether the bus used for our school trip was bodied by Strachans or Northern Counties I don't know, because Southdown had examples of both. The very first utilities to arrive, Nos 400/1 (GCD 974/5), carried lowbridge bodies by Northern Counties. These were followed by three with Strachans lowbridge bodies and three with highbridge bodies by the same bodybuilder. From then on bodywork was divided between Park Royal, Weymann and Northern Counties. Northern Counties was given dispensation to build metal-framed bodies, the others being composite. In many cases the latter were built using unseasoned timber which led to early withdrawal or rebodying. There was little doubt, in my eyes, that the Strachans product was the least attractive; in fact the lowbridge versions were probably the ugliest buses ever to carry the Southdown fleetname.

Exactly 100 Guys were delivered from 1943 to 1946, and there were many variations. When delivered, around 40 had wooden slatted seats, whilst others arrived in green and grey or all-over grey livery. This seems to have been due to the combination of a shortage of paint and an attempt to make the buses less conspicuous from the air. For the latter reason, those retaining Southdown livery were given dark green roofs. Engines, too, varied between batches, some having the 7-litre Gardner 5LW unit, others being fitted with the larger, 8.4-litre 6LW. The latter required an extended bonnet to accommodate its extra length, which actually took the chassis above the maximum legal overall length by some nine inches. After the war a fair amount of engine swapping took place, some buses having their 5LW units replaced by the larger 6LW and *vice versa*, although the reason for this is not entirely clear.

In 1949 a rebuilding programme was started on the Northern Counties bodies, their metal frames being expected to lead to longer life. The rebuilding was carried out by Southdown itself and included the fitting of side destination indicators and fixed front upper-deck windows. In 1951 the Strachans and Northern Counties lowbridge bodies were replaced by East Lancs highbridge bodies removed from withdrawn prewar TDs. Although built in 1943, the East Lancs product showed few signs of austerity specification,

◄ No 489 (GUF 389), a 1945 Weymann-bodied Guy Arab, demonstrates the later postwar livery with four dark green lines which greatly enhanced its appearance. It is seen near Edward Street, Brighton, on a local route. The highbridge 'H' can just be seen under the fleetnumber at the rear offside. *W. J. Haynes / Southdown Enthusiasts' Club*

being little different from the bodybuilder's postwar product. When fitted with the usual Southdown moquette seating and painted in full fleet livery, there was little to indicate to the average passenger that the Guys were anything other than a normal Southdown bus.

At about the same time, Southdown decided to extend its open-top services. Permission had been granted for open-top double-deckers to run to the Top of Beachy Head, and other services were planned for the Portsmouth and Worthing areas. The utility Guys presented themselves as suitable vehicles for conversion. The first to be so treated was 409 (GUF 69), a Park Royal-bodied example, which underwent a comprehensive conversion. The roof and upper-deck windows having been removed, the front and rear of the upper deck were built up to a curved profile, with the

waistrail above the driver's cab similarly curved to match. The usual beading which carried the dark green lining was replaced by aluminium strips with dark green inserts, and the destination screen was given an aluminium surround. Aluminium beading was also fitted as a surround to the mudguards, and front wheel-rings were fitted. The bus emerged in the livery carried by the ageing open-top TD1s, which was cream with apple-green waistband and apple green below the lower-deck windows, but subsequent conversions carried standard livery, and 409 was subsequently repainted to match. 'Southdown' script fleetnames, normally reserved for coaches, were carried. There were three types of open-top conversion, the second lacking the wheel-rings and having a straight waistline above the driver's cab, whilst the third was a much plainer affair with normal dark green lining in

Open-top conversions of the Guy Arabs in the 1950s ousted the open-top Leyland TD1s. No 446 (GUF 146) represents the conversion of the 1945 Park Royal-bodied examples. With a good load on board, it approaches Devil's Dyke on the final leg of the long 102 route through the South Downs from Worthing. Classic British-built cars, in the shape of a 100E Ford Prefect, Triumph Herald and Austin A35, make for interesting comparisons.
Photobus

place of the aluminium beading, but having a front upper-deck windscreen. In this form some reached the grand old age of 20 — not bad for a utility Guy with original body, albeit much rebuilt.

Impressed by the economy and rugged reliability of the wartime Guy, many operators came back for more after the cessation of hostilities. In fact some, such as Chester and East Kent, adopted the Arab as their standard postwar double-decker. Southdown didn't go that far — its love affair with Leyland was too strong for that — but it did have a mild flirtation with the Arab during the late 'Forties and 'Fifties.

In 1948, hard on the heels of 80 PD2s, came 12 Arab IIIs which, like many of the utilities, carried Northern Counties bodywork. They were very different from their wartime counterparts, however, with heavily-radiused corners to the tops of the front and rear upper-deck windows. A low bonnet-line enabled the lower edge of the windscreen to be straight in London 'RT' fashion. Only the protruding bonnet necessitated by the length of the Gardner 6LW engine marred the attractive appearance of these buses.

Numbered 500-11 (JCD 500-11), the Arab IIIs were divided between Brighton and Portsmouth, and I can never remember

seeing them in any other areas. Brighton's allocation usually worked along with the utility Guys on local services to Moulsecoomb, Bevendean and Coldean, although they did venture further inland to Chailey, Golden Cross, Horsham and even Tunbridge Wells. One of Brighton's allocation was 502, which had been exhibited at the 1948 Commercial Motor Show and which differed considerably from the rest of the batch. The front and rear windows were even more heavily radiussed at both top and bottom, the destination screens had chrome surrounds and the lower deck was fitted with 'standee' windows. Like a number of other Northern Counties-bodied vehicles taken into the Southdown fleet from time to time, 502 featured a patent heating and ventilation system. The JCD-registered Arabs were always favourites of mine. In the early 'Sixties I moved to Patcham and, for the first time in my life, had a bus route passing the front door. Moreover, it was one of the usual haunts of the JCD Guys. Deep joy! It was short-lived, however, for a month later the service was diverted and my days of bus-spotting from the bedroom window ceased abruptly!

It was seven years before a further batch of 12 Guys was delivered. These were 512-23 (OUF 512-23) and were Arab IVs with handsome Park Royal bodies identical to those on the OCD-registered Leyland PD2s delivered in the same year. They bore an obvious resemblance to the London RT, with gracefully curved frontal profile and deep, half-drop windows, but, whereas other operators had been specifying vehicles of four-bay construction for some years, Southdown clung stubbornly to its preference for five bays. Brighton's allocation was put to work on the longer inland routes, such as the 17 to Horsham and the 23 to Crawley.

The following year (1956) saw the arrival of no fewer than 36 Arab IVs — 524-59 (PUF 624-59) — which, to my mind, were the *crème de la crème* and which figure highly in my list of all-time favourite buses. They were virtually identical to the OUFs but had sliding vents instead of half-drop windows, giving them a much neater appearance. They were, in fact, the first

Southdown double-deckers to be so equipped. The Brighton allocation was put to work on the trunk route 12 to Eastbourne, but only for about a year until they were replaced by new East Lancs- and Beadle-bodied PD2/12s; they then joined the OUFs on the longer inland routes throughout the area.

As an errant schoolboy, when I tired of logarithms and French verbs I would play truant. No amusement arcades for me, though; I would take a bus ride! Occasionally I would try the marathon four-hour 122 service to Gravesend or the 31 to Portsmouth, but my favourite jaunt was to Eastbourne, travelling by Guy on service 25 via Lewes, Berwick and Polegate and returning via the coast road on service 12, the vehicle for which would be a Leyland PD2/12 with either Beadle or East Lancs body. I could never quite make up my mind which of the types I preferred but, being a Gardner fan, the Arab usually won by a short radiator. For me both types represented the peak of British bus design. From then on it all started to go downhill. However, Joe Public is a fickle fellow, and, handsome, reliable and comfortable though the Guys undoubtedly were, they did not always find favour with him.

Just after the delivery of the OUF batch there was a national rail strike. To cope with the tremendous increase in traffic (this was the mid-'Fifties, remember) the brand-new Arabs, together with some of their PD2 counterparts, were put to work on the Brighton–London express service. Complaints were rife! 'We booked to travel by coach, not bus!' How nice it would have been to offer them a dual-purpose National instead.

It was reliability for which the Arab was renowned. I remember one of Southdown's Area Engineers of the time telling me that you could 'put a Gardner 6LW in a Guy and forget about it', and that was certainly the impression they gave. On the 25 route to Eastbourne, once Lewes was left behind they would purr along merrily as if they could go on forever. They didn't, of course, and were eventually replaced on the longer services by Leyland PD3s or, more commonly, by 36ft Leopards. A pity. It was never quite the same going for a ride into the country on a single-decker. The slogan 'You see more of the countryside from the top of a bus' no longer applied, and I often wonder how many passengers who travelled for pleasure were lost because of this strategy. The Arab IVs were relegated to town services, particularly in the Worthing area.

The last Guy to remain in service in the Brighton area was 550. One evening, after visiting a friend in Patcham, I made one of those on-the-spot decisions for which there is no logical

explanation: instead of catching the Brighton, Hove & District bus which stopped at the bottom of his road, I walked a mile or so to the A23. I hadn't been waiting long when what should come along but good old 550 working a 117 from Horsham, something the Guys had not done on a regular basis for a very long time. I travelled on it to the centre of Brighton where, instead of running into Pool Valley, it stopped in the Old Steine. By this time I was the only passenger on board. I alighted and, as I walked away, the driver turned off the saloon lights and the bus drove slowly and quietly away towards Edward Street garage. I never saw it again and, although I might be wrong, I like to think I was the last person to ride on a Guy in Brighton.

No 550 and many others ended up in Hong Kong, where they suffered all sorts of indignities. Thankfully, 547 would be preserved and beautifully restored and, on certain running days, it is possible to ride on it and be reminded of what superb vehicles they were.

Such was the speed of progress in the immediate postwar years that it is hard to believe that a mere three years spanned the delivery of the last 'Utilities' and Arab III No 500 (JCD 500), seen at speed near Fareham with a Standard van in hot pursuit. These were the days when tobacco companies would swell the revenue of Southdown with their advertising. *W. J. Haynes / Southdown Enthusiasts' Club*

4. E181 — THE TANK ENGINE

By the time hostilities ceased in 1945, most British bus fleets were in a sorry state. Spare parts had been difficult to obtain, and in any case only essential maintenance had been carried out. Many buses had by far exceeded their expected life-span, whilst others were in need of rebuilding or rebodying, and even the utilities delivered during the war needed modifications to bring them up to acceptable peacetime standards.

Coachbuilders, in particular, were inundated with work — so much so that, as has already been mentioned, Southdown's '1400' class Tigers were rebuilt by a number of unlikely concerns,

including various aviation companies. The same pattern was being repeated all over the country, and the result was the springing-up of countless new bodybuilding concerns, most of which lasted only until the early or mid-'Fifties.

As far as chassis were concerned, most manufacturers were hell-bent on producing as many as possible, and stuck largely to their prewar designs. The exception was Leyland Motors Ltd.

From 1942 to 1945 Leyland had been concerned solely with the production of tanks and military vehicles, and during this time had developed a new 7.4-litre diesel engine for use in the

Pool Valley, Brighton, is the setting for this fine view of 266 (GUF 666). Built in 1946, this bus marked Southdown's return to Leyland for its chassis requirements, being a Titan PD1 with a body by Park Royal which had a 'relaxed utility' look about it. *courtesy of the Omnibus Society*

Matilda tank. In 1946 a new bus chassis was introduced which incorporated this engine, by now designated 'E181'. Although of lower capacity than the prewar 8.6-litre unit, it proved to be more powerful, although it was also noisier, having a harsh beat that left no doubt that it was a diesel. A new gearbox was also designed, and the completed chassis became known as the Titan PD1 (for double-deck use) and Tiger PS1 (for single-deckers).

Southdown was as much in need of new vehicles as everyone else, and in 1946 took delivery of 25 PD1s with Park Royal bodies to what was known as 'relaxed' utility specification. Fleetnumbers followed on from the prewar Titans, being 266-90 (GUF 666-90). (It was quite amazing how, even throughout the war years, Southdown had managed to obtain matching registrations for most of its buses.) The 54-seat composite bodies by Park Royal were based very obviously on that concern's utility design but to a relaxed standard with more subtle curves. They also showed a return to some prewar features such as the shape of the rearmost upper-deck side window and the 'D'-shaped staircase window, although the latter were subsequently panelled over. As delivered, they retained the wartime dark green roofs and had painted radiators, again dark green; they later received chrome radiator shells. A representation of one of these buses in almost original condition was featured on the cover of Southdown's timetable booklets for many years.

In 1947 a further 25 PD1s arrived, this time with Leyland's own all-metal bodywork, which showed a full return to peacetime standards including a cream roof, although they still sported painted radiators, later replaced. They were numbered 291-315 (HCD 891-915).

The E181 engine might have been more powerful than the prewar version but it seemed to leave a lot to be desired, particularly as far as its hill-climbing capabilities were concerned. I remember travelling on one of the Leyland-bodied examples which was acting as a relief on service 12 from Eastbourne to Brighton. Admittedly it had a standing load and admittedly the climb out of Eastbourne is pretty

267 (GUF 667) is seen in the late 1950s at Cavendish Place garage, Eastbourne. By now it has lost its dark green lining in favour of a simpler application of green and cream, but the chrome radiator more than makes up for this. A later 8ft-wide Guy Arab stands alongside, both buses having blinds set for route 15. The classic BSA motorcycle on the right was possibly owned by a Southdown employee. *John Bishop*

Car 315 (HCD 915) was the last of the all-Leyland PD1s to be delivered, in 1947. The dark green radiator would later be chromed to enhance this grand vehicle, but it already looked every inch a Southdown bus when seen in pristine condition in Worthing on the premier 31 route to Portsmouth.
W. J. Haynes / Southdown Enthusiasts' Club

testing, but halfway up the PD1 refused to go any further, and half the passengers had to dismount and follow the bus on foot. How common this kind of occurrence was I don't know, but the PD1s all seemed to end up on fairly flat routes. I particularly associated them with services 9 and 10 from Brighton to Littlehampton and Arundel respectively. My most enduring memory of these buses, however, is of their tickover, which was so slow that one expected the engine to stall at any moment. Whatever their faults, they fulfilled a desperate need when delivered, and continued in Southdown service until 1963/4, many then going on to give further service elsewhere. Four of the Park Royal-bodied examples were sold to Mexborough & Swinton, where they continued to operate in Southdown livery, whilst most of the others found homes with independents.

By 1946 Southdown had received no new coaches or single-deckers for some seven years. The single-deck bus situation was dealt with by rebuilding the '1400' class Leyland Tigers, but the coach fleet was a different matter. Not only were many of the coaches becoming too old for front-line coach work, but replacements were required for the vehicles commandeered by the War Department. The Leyland PS1 was the obvious choice of chassis, and 125 were ordered for delivery from 1947 to 1949. Obtaining bodywork for this significant number was not so easy, and the order had to be spread amongst six coachbuilders.

The first 25 arrived in two batches during 1947 and had bodies by Eastern Coach Works to what was basically its standard postwar design for both single-deck buses and coaches. The coach version was distinguished externally by a stepped 'flash' beneath the windows, which signified that the vehicle was fitted for dual-purpose or express work. Southdown's were probably unique in that ECW's standard sliding vents were removed and replaced by the much-favoured half-drops, in this case spring-loaded with metal frames and of a design that the author at least had not seen on any other vehicle. They looked smart enough with their dark green upper-works, cream flash and apple green below. The design was attractive and the finished vehicles were quite handsome, but there was little disguising the fact that they were based on a bus design and hardly in keeping with the rest of the coach fleet.

Initially they were used solely on express services, but in 1954/5 they were transferred to bus work. The first batch to be converted received bus-style destination-screen boxes front and rear, together with bus seats. The next group to go through the works were fitted with bus screens but retained their coach seats, whilst the remainder were unaltered. Most had their dark green roofs and window surrounds repainted in apple green and a few received bus style fleetnames although most seemed to retain their coach-style script fleetnames. They were originally numbered 1227-51 (GUF 727-46, HCD 447-51) but on transfer to bus work were renumbered in the 600 series — strangely in order of conversion rather than their original number order, which meant that their fleet and registration numbers no longer matched.

The second batch of PS1s — 1252-63 (HCD 852-4, HUF 285, HCD 856-63) — had bodies by Park Royal, a firm not unfamiliar with Southdown's requirements but which decided to build to a design specified by East Kent. They featured a straight roof and waistline and, although they looked quite neat in Southdown livery, they lacked the subtle curves of their contemporaries. A further 13 such coaches were

1947 Leyland Tiger PS1/ECW 679 (GUF 733), previously car 1233, stands on the forecourt of Chichester garage. In 1955/6 Southdown converted a number of the type from coaches to buses, and the addition of destination screens and dark green roofs greatly enhanced the appearance of these already attractive vehicles. The Leyland TD5 in the background, 237 (FUF 237), appears to be looking on enviously! *Eric Surfleet / Glyn Kraemer-Johnson collection*

delivered in 1948, which received fleetnumbers 1299-1311 (HUF 299-311).

Thomas Harrington of Hove, one of Southdown's tried and tested suppliers, built bodies for only six PS1s, 1264-9 (HUF 4-9). At the time, Harrington had developed a heating and ventilation system which required the fitting of a 'dorsal fin' to the rear dome and which made them instantly recognisable. Southdown, however, was not into such gimmicks and declined this option. The resultant coaches had the good looks one had come to expect from this coachbuilder.

Another coachbuilder new to Southdown was Windover, a firm which had specialised in the building of high-class car bodies but had seen the demand for coach bodies as an opportunity to widen its scope. Windover had developed an attractive half-cab body immediately identifiable by the 'tear-drop' mouldings around the wheels. No concession was made to Southdown's requirements, the standard body being supplied. They lacked a canopy over the bonnet and, although not unattractive, remained very much 'odd men out' in the fleet. Only six were supplied, being numbered 1270-5 (HUF 270-5).

Beadle was, of course, no stranger to Southdown and was contracted to build bodies for 23 of the PS1s, these being delivered in 1948/9 as 1276-98 (HUF 276-84, HCD 855, HUF 286-98 — for some reason coaches 1255 and 1285 appear to have each received the registration intended for the other). They were to a slightly modified version of the prewar design and very much to Southdown's requirements.

The final coachbuilder to produce bodies for the PS1s was Duple Motor Bodies. Duple was a very well-known name in the industry but had never before built bodies for Southdown. It obviously had an eye to the future, for it went to great lengths to produce a body that was as close as possible to Southdown's standard for express and private-hire work. The result was a body featuring subtle curves and looking very much a Southdown thoroughbred. The 40 Duple-bodied PS1s, which were to be the

No 1265 (HUF 5), a Leyland Tiger PS1 bodied by Harrington Coachworks, looks every inch a proud Southdown as it prepares to set off from Brighton's Madeira Drive on an excursion to Ashurst Woods and Partridge Green. Surprisingly, 1265 formed one of only a small batch of six, the rest being bodied by Park Royal, Beadle, ECW, Windover and Duple.
W. J. Haynes / Southdown Enthusiasts' Club

No 1329 (HUF 929) shows the Duple body on the Leyland Tiger PS1 chassis, in 'as delivered' condition with painted radiator. The Southdown driver rests after taking his passengers to Windsor and Oxford. The boards on the side have yet to be painted with the coach route or Company advertising.
Glyn Kraemer-Johnson collection

This early-1960s view captures the period, with an Austin Devon to the left and a then new 'Moggy' Minor to the right. A traditional red telephone box and the typical Southdown architecture of Royal Parade garage at Eastbourne provide an attractive backdrop for 1313 (HUF 313), a rebuilt Duple-bodied Leyland Tiger PS1. It stands with boards for the Eastbourne–London service, and proudly shows the Beadle rebuild badge on its front.
John Bishop

last full-size half-cab coaches to be supplied to Southdown, were numbered 1312-51 (HUF 312-26, 927-51) and delivered over a two-year period from 1947 to 1949.

Unfortunately the advent of the underfloor-engined chassis meant that within four or five years the PS1 coaches were becoming outdated. In an effort to prolong their lives and to give them a more modern image, the Beadle and Duple-bodied examples were all sent to Beadle to be rebuilt with full fronts and the bodies lightly modified with different mouldings etc. The resulting vehicles were very similar in appearance to the Beadle rebuilds that were entering service at the same time. Looking back more than 50 years, it is difficult to remember how they appeared at the time, but today, in the author's opinion, they don't look that much more up-to-date and certainly weren't as handsome as they had been in half-cab form. Moreover, the front bulkheads were removed so that, as with the underfloor-engined coaches, the driver was not separated from his passengers, but the downside was that the noise level in the saloon was increased considerably. In this form they lasted until 1960/1.

It is perhaps pertinent to mention here the Beadle rebuilds, which entered service in the 1952-4 period. John C. Beadle of

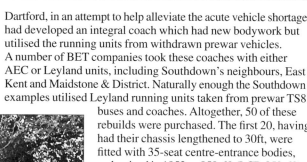

Dartford, in an attempt to help alleviate the acute vehicle shortage, had developed an integral coach which had new bodywork but utilised the running units from withdrawn prewar vehicles. A number of BET companies took these coaches with either AEC or Leyland units, including Southdown's neighbours, East Kent and Maidstone & District. Naturally enough the Southdown examples utilised Leyland running units taken from prewar TS8 buses and coaches. Altogether, 50 of these rebuilds were purchased. The first 20, having had their chassis lengthened to 30ft, were fitted with 35-seat centre-entrance bodies, and arrived in 1952 as 850-69 (LCD 850-69). The remainder were 26ft in length and carried 26 passengers in their forward-entrance bodies; these materialised in 1953/4 as 870-99 (MCD 870-84, MUF 485-92, NCD 93-9). As with their rebuilt PS1 counterparts, attempts to give them a modern appearance failed miserably, but they did fulfil a need as well as ensuring that the roar of the prewar 8.6-litre engine continued to be heard. In later years many were converted to one-man-operated buses, and spent their last days trundling around on some of the more lightly-trafficked routes.

The early 1950s saw a need for more coaches, and the answer was to use perfectly service-able '1400' class Leyland Tigers as the basis for a number of coaches known by enthusiasts as 'Beadle Rebuilds'. No 855 (LCD 855) of 1952 represents the longer version. The 7ft 6in chassis width is readily apparent, the wheels being set well in from the wing of the 8ft-wide body.
Glyn Kraemer-Johnson collection

5. THE PEAK OF BRITISH BUS DESIGN

1948 saw an event that was to shape the Southdown fleet for the next 20 years. This was the introduction by Leyland of its PD2 double-deck chassis. The major difference in this chassis was the use of a larger and more powerful engine of 9.8-litre capacity, together with a synchromesh gearbox, although not all the Southdown examples were fitted with the latter. The engine, known as the O.600, was to power the majority of Southdown's double-deckers until the advent of the rear-engined chassis.

Southdown's first PD2s carried Leyland's own metal-framed bodywork, which was virtually the same as that carried by the HCD-registered PD1s. The body was particularly handsome, with a gently curved front profile. My main memories of the type, however, are of a strange smell that seemed unique to the type, and of large wooden 'notice boards' fixed to the inside of the front dome, which, due to its shape, always reminded me of half an aircraft propeller!

No fewer than 80 PD2/1s were delivered, numbered 316-95 (JCD 16-95), and were put to work on the Company's premier routes such as the 12 (Brighton–Eastbourne) and 31 (Brighton–Southsea), which they maintained until the arrival of the first PD2/12s in the early 'Fifties. The JCDs were very useful workhorses and worked on most services until their withdrawal in the mid 'Sixties, some lasting until 1967.

In 1950 the permitted maximum length and width of double-deckers were increased to 27ft 6in and 8ft respectively. Leyland increased the dimensions of the PD2 accordingly, and the type supplied to Southdown with vacuum brakes was designated PD2/12. The increased dimensions would allow Southdown to increase the seating capacity from 54 to 59 — still a very modest figure compared to some other operators.

The first PD2/12 delivered to Southdown, 700 (KUF 700), was something of an oddity, being an experimental double-deck coach. Northern Counties was chosen to build the body, and No 700 appeared on that firm's stand at the 1950 Commercial Motor Show. It bore some resemblance to the Guys delivered in 1948, especially the experimental 502, but had a full front and coach seats for just 44. It was also Southdown's first and only double-decker to feature four-bay construction (ie four windows between

bulkheads). It featured glass cant panels in the roof, and a received version of the bus livery, having apple-green window surrounds.

No 700 was put to work on the Eastbourne–London service but was not a success. It was almost a ton overweight, which gave it a sluggish performance, particularly when hill-climbing, and rolled so much on corners that even the lower-deck passengers felt ill! Various seating arrangements were tried to overcome the problems, but none succeeded. It was eventually upseated to 50 and allocated to Bognor Regis, where it ended its days on private-hire and schools duties. Unsuccessful it may have been, but there was little doubt that its design laid the foundation for the 'Queen Mary' PD3s which were to follow some eight years later.

Three batches of Leyland-bodied PD2/12s followed in 1951, 1952 and 1953. The body was clearly based on the immediate postwar body as fitted to the JCDs but was widened between bulkheads, with a tapering front when looked at in plan. The corners of the windows were radiused, giving a sleeker appearance. The body was known as the 'Farington', the name being derived from its place of manufacture.

During the late 'Forties and early 'Fifties many coachbuilders were engaged in building bodies for London Transport's 7,000-strong RT family, and it was hardly surprising that features of the RT should influence their own designs. Leyland itself had been contracted to build both bodies and chassis for the 500 RTWs, and, although the basic Leyland design remained unaffected, there were traces of London influence in detail design, certainly

▲ It was predictable that the next batch of buses after the PD1s would be PD2s; 373 (JCD 73), dating from 1948, emerges from Steyne Gardens, Worthing, having travelled down from Horsham. These were the days when there was as much chance of winning the Littlewoods Pools as winning the lottery! *Photobus*

in the case of the Southdown examples. Although many operators specified sliding vents on the Farington body, Southdown stuck to the half-drop variety, although these were now fitted with winding gear rather than being of the none-too-reliable spring-loaded type. Metal louvres over the opening windows only were incorporated into the main body in RT fashion. Internally, instead of varnished woodwork as found on the PD2/1s, the side panels and window frames were covered in rexine — brown to halfway up the window pillars and cream above.

The all-Leyland PD2/12s came in three batches, 701-24 (KUF 701-24), 725-44 (LUF 225-244) and 745-54 (MCD 745-54). 754 had the last Leyland body to be delivered to Southdown and was exhibited at the Festival of Britain in 1951 (the 1950s equivalent of the Millennium Dome!). 701-24 had crash gearboxes whilst the first 32 were delivered with open platforms, power-operated jack-knife doors being fitted by Southdown. All subsequent buses were so equipped from new.

Following Leyland Motors' decision to cease its bodybuilding activities, Southdown turned to Northern Counties for the bodies on its next batch of 10 PD2/12s. 755-64 (MUF 455-64) were to a much more restrained design than had previously emerged from the Wigan factory, the heavily-radiused corners being restricted to the top outside edges of the front upper-deck windows and the rear emergency exit. The resulting vehicles were quite handsome, at least from the front, the rear end somehow managing to look about 10ft wide. Internally, the lower-deck side panels and window pillars were covered in Formica, those upstairs retaining rexine which, bearing in mind nicotine deposits on the upper deck, seemed to be the wrong way round.

Twelve more PD2/12s arrived in 1955 numbered 765-76 (OCD 765-76). This time, Park Royal bodies were fitted, being identical to the bodies carried by the OUF-registered Guys delivered at the same time and bearing a strong resemblance to the RT. Whereas this body, when built for other operators, was usually of four-bay construction, Southdown stuck doggedly to five. Similarly, while most operators were by now specifying sliding vents, Southdown continued to choose half-drops which, in the case of the Park Royal body, increased its likeness to the RT. Although they made very handsome buses, the Park Royal bodies on both Leyland and Guy chassis had a high and very curved lower edge to the front bulkhead windows. This appeared to have been designed with the AEC Regent V in mind, but on other chassis (particularly the Arab) was unnecessarily high and restricted forward visibility.

A final 36 PD2/12s were delivered in 1956/7 and were numbered 777-812 (RUF 177-212). The first 12 had bodies by Southdown's old ally, Beadle of Dartford, which was busy bodying coaches for the Company at the time. They were the first double-deckers to be built by Beadle for some years and were sadly also to be the last, for Beadle was shortly to close down the coachbuilding side of its business and concentrate on car sales. Nos 777-88 were actually built on Park Royal frames and were almost identical to the Park Royal bodies on the PUF-registered Guys, being fitted (at last!) with sliding vents. Both these bodies and those on the PUFs lacked a side destination screen. Later in life the rear destination screens were painted over, leaving just a route number at the back — a real come-down after the elaborate screen displays fitted in the 'Thirties. The final batch, 24 in number, carried handsome bodywork by East Lancs with a frontal profile that was slightly more upright than on the Park Royal body and which, in the author's opinion, marked the zenith of British bus design. They featured hefty sliding platform doors, which suffered less from rattles and draughts than the jack-knife variety but which, when the bus was parked on an incline, would open with a series of judders and clunks! One of this batch, 805, survives in preservation; together with Park Royal-bodied 772 and Guy Arab 547, it often appears at the various running days, so one can still salivate over the ultimate in British bus design.

6. THE TIGER AND HER CUB

With the introduction of the underfloor-engined single-decker, most of the major manufacturers produced rugged heavyweights. Leyland and AEC brought out their Royal Tiger and Regal IV respectively. Without much imagination for model names, Guy built the Arab UF and Dennis the Lancet UF, whilst Daimler introduced the Freeline. Bristol was the only manufacturer to eschew the heavyweight chassis and entered the field with its LS ('Light Saloon'). However, at this time Bristol products were only available to the nationalised companies.

In the South East, the BET companies all opted for the Leyland Royal Tiger except for Aldershot & District, which bought a solitary Dennis Dominant and then waited for the lightweights.

Given its long association with Leyland, it was hardly surprising that Southdown should show the most enthusiasm for the new model. Whereas the Royal Tigers delivered to its neighbours had all been PSU1/15 models fitted with coach bodies, Southdown also took a number of PSU1/13s for bus work. Ordered to replace the Company's ageing fleet of prewar Tigers, an initial batch of 10 was delivered in 1952 as 1500-9 (LUF 500-9). Fitted with 40 seat bodies by East Lancs, they were eye-catchingly modern at the time but included features that, by today's standards, seem very dated. For instance, this first batch had rear entrances. The combination of an underfloor engine and a rear entrance now seems eccentric to say the least, but in 1952 there was no question of dispensing with the conductor. Eccentric or not, they held a great fascination for an 11-year-old schoolboy, for, if you were lucky you could 'bag' the front seat and not only have an excellent view ahead, uninterrupted by bonnet and mudguards, but would also be sitting next to the driver whose cab was not enclosed and who, if you were very, very lucky, might even speak to you. If he did, you might find out some inside information about new vehicles or forthcoming deliveries!

Beneath the rear windows was a destination screen as large and informative as that at the front, showing route number, destination and 'via' points in the same manner as the prewar Tigers they were replacing. In addition there was a route-number screen beside the door, which was a hand-operated sliding affair. The vehicles had a high waistrail that resulted in shallow windows; it may have been an optical illusion, but those in the rear half of the body seemed narrower than those at the front. All opening windows were of the winding half-drop variety. The waistband mouldings dipped in a curved 'V' shape at the front — a feature of Southdown single-deckers for some time to come. The driver's windscreen was angled and recessed in RF fashion, whilst the nearside windscreen was flush-fitting and of one piece. Internally, the buses were finished to the usual Southdown standard, with the familiar brown moquette on seat backs and cushions. Side panels were covered in brown rexine to halfway up the window pillars, with cream above.

In 1953 a further 30 Royal Tiger buses were delivered. Numbered 1510-39 (MCD 510-39), they were similar in most respects to the earlier batch, the most noticeable difference being the entrance position, which had moved to the centre and was fitted with a power-operated sliding door. The nearside windscreen was also recessed to match the offside.

▲ The early 1950s saw the advent of the underfloor engine, and Southdown was not slow to purchase the Leyland Royal Tiger to fulfil its needs for replacement of earlier stock. No 1500 (LUF 500), with rear-entrance East Lancs body, is seen at Pool Valley, Brighton, soon after delivery in 1952. *Glyn Kraemer-Johnson collection.*

Car 1635 (LUF 635), an all-Leyland Royal Tiger, appears to have seen better days when photographed at Pool Valley in the 1960s, having been demoted to bus work with an 'add on' destination screen; as if to add insult to injury, it is deemed fit only for relief duty! In the background, a Park Royal-bodied Leyland PD2 swings in from Portsmouth. *John Bishop*

In later life, all 40 were converted to front-entrance layout for one-man operation; at the same time the MCDs lost their recessed nearside windscreens to avoid obstructing the entrance. Also gone, of course, was that opportunity to sit next to the driver. (Strange as it may seem, I cannot remember ever being able to 'see the join' on these conversions as one can on rebuilds of modern buses from dual- to single-door configuration.) Later still, their dark green roofs were painted apple green.

In addition to the service buses, Southdown bought no fewer than 115 Royal Tigers for coach work. First to arrive, in 1951, were 10 with curvaceous but heavy-looking Duple Ambassador bodywork. All the early bodies for underfloor-engined single-deckers seemed to suffer from the same fault — a high waistrail that resulted in shallow windows — and the Duple Ambassador was no exception. As for looking heavy, they weighed in at over eight tons, equal to the weight of a London RT. The roofline was curved, as was the waistrail, the latter drooping at the front only to curve upwards again beneath the windscreen. Two small destination screens were fitted beneath the windscreen, also curved, and below them decorative aluminium strips, the lowest of which formed a triangle in which a Southdown badge replaced that of the Royal Tiger. This decorative moulding, together with the curved beading on the side panels, was to become a distinctive feature of almost all Southdown coaches throughout the 'Fifties. They were fitted with glass cant panels, centre entrances and only 26 seats for use on extended tours, which were rapidly becoming an important part of Southdown's business. Originally numbered 800-9 (LCD 200-9), they were later renumbered 1800-9 to make way for new PD2 double-deckers.

A further 20 Royal Tigers followed in 1952, again with 26 seats for touring work but this time with bodies by Harrington, which produced a much more elegant-looking coach. Numbered 810-29 (LUF 810-29), they later became 1810-29. The Harrington body was also fairly rounded, but the curves were much gentler than those of the Ambassador, resulting in a much more stylish vehicle. Glass cant panels were again fitted to give passengers a superior view when travelling in mountainous country. Delivered in the usual all-over apple-green livery, they later had their upper parts painted cream, which gave them a more distinctive appearance.

Still in 1952, a further 20 Royal Tigers were delivered. These were numbered 1600-19 (LUF 600-19) and were again fitted with Duple Ambassador 41-seat bodies for excursion and private-hire work. Following severe accident damage, the last of these was rebodied with a later style of body featuring a modified front end: two small windows were incorporated above the windscreen in the same manner as the Harrington-bodied examples, and the tops of the foremost side windows were angled upwards, which helped to remove the 'drooping' look.

Still more Royal Tigers followed in the shape of 1620-44 (LUF 620-44). These were completely different from earlier examples, having Leyland's own coach body, and were the first 'off-the-peg' coaches bought since the Windover- and ECW-bodied PS1s of the late 'Forties. They could hardly have differed more from the Duple-bodied Tigers: whereas the Ambassador

had barely a straight line in its design, it was equally difficult to find a curved one on the Leyland body — the roof and waistline were completely straight. The windscreen was angled outwards with a chrome surround and smaller windows beneath the windscreen and the front side windows. The curved mouldings on the front dash that had become something of a Southdown trademark were straightened into a triangle with a Southdown badge in its centre. Internally, the usual Southdown moquette was used, but the seats themselves were not standard, having a grab-rail incorporated into the seatbacks. They were intended for express work and I particularly remember them as regular performers on the South Coast Express service. In later life many were converted for bus work through the fitting of a large destination screen on the front dome. They retained their centre entrances, which made them unsuitable for one-man operation, and seemed highly impractical; somehow, they never seemed to fit in happily with the rest of the fleet. Theirs were, incidentally, the only single-deck Leyland bodies ever purchased by Southdown.

Five more Royal Tigers were delivered in 1953 with what were called Duple 'Coronation Ambassador' bodies. Although basically to the Ambassador design they had different front-end styling and a heavily embellished waistband that Southdown painted cream, giving some welcome relief to the all-over green normally employed. Centre entrances were again specified for these 41-seaters, which were numbered 1645-9 (MCD 45-9).

Two further touring coaches were delivered in 1953, and another three in 1955, which showed a return to Harrington coachwork. Numbered 1830-4 (MUF 430/1, OUF 832-4), these and all subsequent Royal Tigers were based on the PSU1/16 chassis, a refined version of the PSU1/15 previously specified for Southdown coaches. Nos 1832-4 were noteworthy in being only 7ft 6in wide, a fact taken possibly into consideration when

1832/3 were transferred to the Ulster Transport Authority for exclusive use on Southdown tours in Northern Ireland.

For some reason the final 30 Royal Tigers reverted to the Duple Ambassador body rather than the more elegant Coronation Ambassador. All had 41-seat centre-entrance coachwork, and they were numbered 1650-9 (MUF 650-9), 1661-8 (NCD 661-8) and 1669-80 (NUF 69-80). (The 'missing' number, 1660, was the new identity of the aforementioned rebodied No 1619.) Thus ended Southdown's huge intake of Royal Tigers, comprising 115 coaches and 40 buses.

It was not long before the manufacturers realised that their first underfloor-engined chassis were over-engineered and unnecessarily heavy, with consequent effects on fuel consumption. This was a time when bus operators were beginning to look more closely at running costs, and so the three 'big boys' — AEC, Guy and Leyland — all saw fit to introduce new lightweight chassis. AEC brought out its Reliance, and Guy the Arab LUF, while Leyland's Royal Tiger begat the Tiger Cub.

The Tiger Cub was displayed at the 1952 Commercial Motor Show, the same as that at which Southdown's Royal Tiger 1645 appeared. It was a full-size (30ft) chassis powered by Leyland's O.350 5.7-litre engine, as used in the Comet goods range. At first only a bus chassis was available, but a coach chassis followed in 1953 with the engine uprated to develop 108bhp at 2,400rpm, as compared with the bus version which was set to develop 90bhp at 2,200rpm.

Although three of the four BET operators in the South East had bought the Royal Tiger, only Southdown showed interest in its lightweight offspring, the Tiger Cub. First to arrive were 20 PSUC1/1 (bus) chassis with 39-seat front-entrance bodies by a little-known concern, Nudd Bros & Lockyer, which was in fact a subsidiary of the Duple group; the batch was numbered 620-39 (MUF 620-39). The 'V'-shaped moulding beneath the windscreen, together with the front bumper and downward curve of the waistrail beneath the cab window, gave them a superficial likeness to the '1500' class Royal Tigers, but there any similarity ended. They had a strange arrangement of opening windows, being a mixture of sliding vents — something new to Southdown, although widely used elsewhere — and quarter-drop winding windows of the type fitted to London Transport's RF and RM classes. The seating, too, was quite non-standard. Although the usual brown moquette was used, the seats themselves were low-backed with a curved top rail — again, a strange choice, considering that the usual 'shaped'

higher-backed seats were fitted to double-deckers delivered at the same time. When new the Tiger Cubs had dark green roofs, but these were later painted apple green. Later still, along with some of the Royal Tigers, they were given cream roofs, which has been reported as a dual-purpose livery, although the interiors hardly lived up to this description.

Five more PSUC1/1s were delivered in 1955, this time with bodies by Park Royal and numbered 640-4 (OUF 640-3, PUF 844). To the same basic design as the Nudd Bros body, the Park Royal differed in that the downward curve of the waistline below the driver's window was convex rather than concave. The small rearmost side window on the Nudd body had also disappeared. Otherwise there was little difference, the same variety of opening windows being fitted.

No further single-deck buses were received until 1962, when a final batch of 10 Tiger Cubs arrived, fitted this time with Marshall 45-seat bodies. Apart from the 'V'-shaped moulding beneath the windscreen they were virtually to the standard (and rather severe) BET design. Sliding vents were fitted, and the seats were covered in the new green moquette, as introduced on PD3s from 1959. Numbered 655-64 (7655-64 CD), they represented a transitional phase in the development of the Southdown single-decker and, perhaps as a result, never quite fitted in with the rest of the fleet.

Whilst Southdown's intake of Tiger Cub service buses was fairly low, this was amply compensated for by the number of coaches purchased. The coach fleet had been largely replaced since the war, firstly by Tiger PS1s and later by underfloor-engined Royal Tigers. The PS1s were only between six and eight years old, but their exposed radiators and half-cab layout meant that by 1955 they were rapidly becoming obsolete and were certainly old-fashioned in passengers' eyes. As previously mentioned, this was partially overcome by having the Duple- and Beadle-bodied examples rebuilt with full fronts, thus giving them a more modern (but less aesthetic) appearance. This only partially resolved the problem, however, and the influx of new coaches continued.

Following on from the large number of Royal Tigers, Southdown turned to the lighter Tiger Cub bodied mostly by Beadle, which produced a design unique to Southdown. This resembled the Duple Ambassador, with curved roof and waistline (these being straight on the standard Beadle product). Side and front mouldings, too, were similar to those on the Ambassador, giving the vehicles a true Southdown appearance.

The first batch of 40 delivered in 1955 started a new numbering series at 1000, being numbered 1000-39 (OUF 100-39), and had centre entrances. Seven were 37-seaters for Southdown's newly introduced Beacon tours. These were cheaper than the Luxury Extended tours and were centred in one resort, with excursions each day. The hotels were of a slightly lower grade and the coaches were less luxurious, having conventional two-plus-two seating, albeit with increased legroom. The remaining 33 vehicles seated 41, for excursion and private-hire work. All had half-drop windows with glass louvres, and the small toplights above the windscreen as featured on the Royal Tigers.

A further 35 similar coaches were delivered in 1956 as 1040-74 (RUF 40-74). These retained the centre entrance, but the windscreens were one-piece and, for the first time on a Southdown coach, sliding ventilators were fitted, these having been adopted on double-deckers at the same time. All were 41-seaters. The following year saw the arrival of another 40 Tiger Cubs — 1075-1114 (SUF 875-914) — which were identical to the RUF-registered batch except that 1091-3 were 37-seaters. Nos 1097-1102 were painted in the blue and cream livery of Triumph Coaches, a Portsmouth-based company recently taken over by Southdown and whose identity was being retained.

A final batch of 15 was delivered in 1958 as 1115-29 (UCD 115-29), these having front entrances. The rear edge of the window in the door and the forward edge of the front side window were curved in the same manner as Beadle's contemporary Rochester design, which, together with the curved waistrail, made for a very attractive coach. Again, seating capacities varied, 1120-5 seating 37 and 1128/9 a mere 32; 1124/5 had their seating reduced to 32 in 1960. No 1128 was used by the Brighton & Hove Albion football team, whilst 1129 was painted in the blue livery of Swedish operator Linjebuss and was used exclusively on that company's British tours. Nos 1126/7, meanwhile, were two further coaches painted in Triumph livery. This batch marked the end of a long association between Southdown and Beadle, as the coachbuilder ceased production shortly after this delivery.

The last two batches of Tiger Cubs to be received carried Weymann Fanfare bodywork. Weymann's coach bodies were never really popular, and the Fanfare probably clocked up more sales than any other. It seemed a strange choice for Southdown, which, after the closure of Beadle, might have been expected to return to its old ally, Harrington. The Weymann Fanfare had been supplied to a number of BET operators, mostly on AEC Reliance chassis, but I have always thought that its choice by Southdown was due to its strong resemblance to the Beadle Rochester, at the front end at least. There were two batches: 1130-44 (XUF 130-44), 37-seaters delivered in 1960, and 1145-54 (8145-54 CD), which arrived in 1962, the first five having 37 seats, the remainder 41. The Weymann Fanfare-bodied Tiger Cubs were very attractive vehicles, even if no concession was made to distinguish them from other operators' Fanfares. They had cream window surrounds and dark green skirts, and featured the new green moquette being used in contemporary PD3 double-deckers.

I always had a soft spot for the Tiger Cub coaches. In the mid-'Fifties I enjoyed two of Southdown's Beacon tours — the first to the Derbyshire Peak District on 1012, the second to North Wales on 1014. Both were thoroughly enjoyable and the vehicles most comfortable, even if they weren't up to the standard of their Royal Tiger brethren. I also travelled on several half-day excursions on the RUF- and SUF-registered batches, always trying to 'bag' the front seat next to the driver!

In all, there were 155 Tiger Cub coaches and 55 buses delivered to Southdown. One of the Weymann Fanfare-bodied examples, 1141, lives on in preservation, but regrettably there are no confirmed survivors from amongst the Beadle examples — particularly sad, as they were unique to Southdown.

'Triumph Coaches' T1097 (SUF 897) basks in the sunshine under the trolleybus wires of Portsmouth. There is, however, no disguising the Southdown ownership of this Beadle-bodied Leyland Tiger Cub of 1957, with its traditional boards on the roof. The 'T' prefix to the fleet-number denoted Triumph in much the same way as it did the Tramocar fleet in Worthing almost 20 years earlier. *John Bishop*

Few buses achieve cult status. Those that do, such as the RT and Routemaster, are generally London vehicles, but Southdown's 'Queen Mary' Leyland PD3s certainly fall into this category. At the risk of being lynched, I'll say that I've never understood what arouses such passions. To me they've always had an unhappy appearance with their down-turned bonnet-lines and fish-mouth grilles. Had they been half-cabs they would have been very handsome, but I'm obviously in the minority!

The maximum legal length for two-axle double-deckers had been increased to 30ft in 1956. Leyland reacted by introducing the PD3 — simply a lengthened version of the PD2. At about the same time it began to fit a straight-through exhaust system, so most PD3s (and PD2s built after 1958) had a more rasping exhaust note. Southdown's choice was for the PD3/4 with synchromesh gearbox. The trend at the time was for larger vehicles and reduced frequencies, the theory being that the same number of seats was available to the passenger. Whilst many operators were introducing rear-engined buses with seating capacities around 78, Southdown, conventional to the last, opted for PD3s seating a modest 69.

From 1958 to 1967 Southdown took delivery of no fewer than 285 PD3s, all with forward-entrance bodies by Northern Counties. Southdown's one concession to modernity was to specify a full front, which bore some resemblance to that on the unsuccessful 700 and gave the buses a rather sad appearance. Standard parts were used for the body, the extra length being achieved by the addition of a half-bay amidships in similar fashion to London's RMLs. One thing the full front did achieve was to bring the new buses to the attention of the general public, who at least realised that the PD3s were different from the prewar Titans! They were quickly nicknamed 'Queen Marys' due to their extra length.

It was usual for new buses to be put to work on services 12 or 31 but, much to the disappointment of Brighton

enthusiasts, the first PD3s, delivered in 1958, were allocated to Portsmouth for use on local routes. Numbered 813-27 (TCD 813-27), they had the Northern Counties trademark of heavily-radiused top corners to the front upper-deck windows (which, if anything, made them look even sadder), and sliding vents were fitted to all but the foremost side windows. The rear lower-deck side windows were curved to match those on the upper deck and sliding vents were shaped to fit. At about this time Southdown modified its livery and these were the first new vehicles to be delivered without the dark green lining.

Over the course of the next nine years a further 10 batches of PD3s were delivered, all differing from the previous one, so that the last to be delivered bore little resemblance to their 1958 counterparts. Sometimes the differences were only minor. For instance the next batch — 828-42 (VUF 828-42) —saw the introduction of a new and rather drab green moquette in place of the traditional Southdown brown, whilst the 1960 deliveries — 843-62 (XUF 843-62) — introduced 'push-out' vents on the front upper-deck windows, which cheered up their appearance a little. Some of these buses were delivered to Brighton, but were again used initially only on local routes.

1961 saw the arrival of a further 50 Queen Marys — 863-912 (2863-2912 CD) — which, with one exception, differed little from the XUFs. The odd man out was 863, a 1960 Commercial Motor Show exhibit, which was fitted with fluorescent lighting and an illuminated offside advertisement panel. These were also features of the 1962 intake, 913-52 (6913-52 CD). The illuminated advert panel was one of those 'fads' for which the bus industry is famous, and never caught on. With a few odd exceptions, the main advertiser to utilise these spaces was Commercial Union Insurance, most of the other vehicles proclaiming 'Better travel by Southdown'. All subsequent deliveries featured fluorescent lighting but, unlike many operators, Southdown did not modify any earlier vehicles, these retaining tungsten lighting to the end. The major difference in the 1962 batch, however, was in the chassis itself, which was of type PD3/5, with pneumocyclic semi-automatic gearbox. Although this variant was apparently successful elsewhere, Southdown's examples seemed very sluggish in comparison with the PD3/4s, and most ended up working on the flatter terrain in and around Portsmouth.

Almost two years passed before the next arrivals, which showed a return to the PD3/4 chassis and conventional gearbox. Nos 953-77 (953-77 CUF) were again equipped with illuminated advert panels, and introduced twin headlights. Following the introduction of new legislation, some of this batch were converted for one-man operation, although they only seem to have been used as such on school duties. The main identifying feature of the converted buses was a reversing window fitted in the rear emergency exit door.

By this time, the Guy open-toppers had reached the end of their life-span and replacements were needed. Instead of carrying out further conversions, Southdown ordered 25 PD3s with convertible Northern Counties bodies. Numbered in the same series as the withdrawn Guys, 400-24 (400-24 DCD) were easily recognisable by their shallower and flatter roofs and the thick beading below the upper-deck windows where the two parts met. Internally, the upper-deck seats were covered in green rexine with pale green Formica backs; side panels were painted brown. Otherwise they were the same as their closed-top counterparts, and operated as such during the winter months.

Delivered in 1965, the next batch were, in the author's opinion, probably the nicest of all the PD3s. They started a new numbering series, being 250-84 (BUF 250-84C), and introduced a new interior. Seats were covered in a new, brighter moquette in various shades of green and fawn, whilst seat backs and side panels were of dark wood-grain Formica. One of this batch, 257, was another to be fitted with an experimental heating and ventilation system. The radiator was housed under the stairs, which allowed a double-curvature windscreen to be fitted, the lower edge of which was straight. The rest of the bus was to the standard design, which made the modern front look rather incongruous. It seemed to spend most of its life on services 9 and 10 (Brighton–Worthing–Littlehampton). A further five convertibles followed the same year, as 425-9 (BUF 425-9C).

Windows were the next area to receive attention, 1966 deliveries 285-314 (FCD 285-314D) being fitted with Auster Rotavents. These consisted of a rotating aluminium tube fitted inside a fixed one, both having apertures which, when lined up, allowed fresh air to enter the vehicle. Unfortunately, later in life, the rotating part became sloppy and tended to drop open of its own accord.

The first of the next batch was delivered early. No 315 (GUF 250D) was one of the few Southdown buses whose registration and fleet numbers did not match. It was also another Earls Court exhibit, appearing at the 1966 Commercial Motor

Show, and had yet another experimental heating and ventilation system. Again, the radiator was beneath the stairs, allowing a double-curvature windscreen to be fitted, but this time a wrap-around window was fitted at the front of the upper deck. Panoramic side windows were also fitted, there being only two main windows on the lower-deck. In some ways the body on 315 was more modern than many rear-engined vehicles entering service at the same time, and yet it looked dated from the start. Its main failing aesthetically was that it was too short to have panoramic windows, and the curved rear lower-deck windows looked particularly out of date. When painted in NBC livery it looked even worse, there being no room on the front for white relief. Rotavents were again fitted.

No 315's basic body design was perpetuated on the final delivery of 24 PD3s received in 1967; for obvious reasons 346-69 (HCD 346-69E) became known as the 'Panoramics'. The major difference was that these buses had conventional radiators, and therefore retained the original two-piece front windscreen with curved lower edges. An attempt was made to make this less incongruous by painting the apple green straight across the front of the bus instead of following the curve of the windscreen. Due to the wrap-around front window and the none-too-effective Rotavents, ventilation on the top deck proved inadequate, so one opening vent was taken from the front upper-deck of each of the 1964 convertible PD3s and fitted in the centre of the front dome on the 'Panoramics'. This seemed to cure the problem, although the convertibles were left with a 'one-eyed' look.

The majority of the later PD3s (from 953 onwards) remained with the Company long enough to receive NBC livery, most from the earlier batches having been sold for further service in Hong Kong. The 'Queen Marys' obviously proved very popular with enthusiasts and, considering the number built, the proportion now in preservation is surprisingly high. It would seem safe to say that we shall be able to continue riding on them for many years to come.

▲ The convertible PD3s were instantly recognisable in closed-top form by the heavy beading below the upper-deck windows. This shot of 407 (407 DCD) passing a Brighton Corporation Leyland PD2/37 in Old Steine shows the 'one eyed' effect these vehicles gained after donating the front offside upper-deck opening vent to the 'panoramic' PD3s. *R. M. J. Maryan/Southdown Enthusiasts' Club*

8. THE YEARS OF THE LEOPARD

By 1961 the coach cruising fleet of Royal Tigers was between eight and 10 years old, which was considered elderly for front-line touring coaches. For replacements Southdown turned to the newly introduced Leyland Leopard, which was in effect a Tiger Cub with O.600 engine and synchromesh gearbox. For the bodies the Company turned to its old ally, Harrington of Hove, which had just introduced its classic Cavalier design.

If the East Lancs PD2s and Park Royal Guys represented the peak of double-deck design then the Cavalier was the zenith of the British coach. It was modern yet restrained, with a gently curving roof and waistline. Carefully placed forward-sloping pillars and mouldings gave an impression of forward motion. Glass cant panels in the roof ensured a light and airy interior, a feeling reinforced by the two-plus-one seating. In Southdown's livery of apple green with cream roof and window surrounds and dark green skirt even the adjective 'beautiful' was not too strong. Fifty-two on Leopard L2T chassis were delivered over a three-year period, all with 28-seat bodies for touring work. Later in life their cream upper-works were repainted apple green, which only slightly marred their handsome looks. It took the National Bus Company's all-over white to ruin their appearance completely. The last five delivered in 1963 were prototypes for the Grenadier

design that was to follow, having longer fixed side windows and forced ventilation, and lacking the glass roof panels.

1962 saw the first 36-footers enter the fleet. These were again Leyland Leopards, but were classified PSU3/3RT and carried unusual Weymann Castillian bodies. The Castillian was in effect a lengthened version of the Fanfare but somehow nowhere near as attractive. The first batch to be delivered, 1155-9 (8155-9 CD), had small side windows with Auster opening vents as fitted to the Fanfares, and seated 49. The second batch, 1160-74 (160-74 AUF) had larger non-opening main windows (four each side) and featured forced ventilation. The fixed windows seemed to make the design even less attractive. They were a mixture of 45- and 49-seaters. 1962 also saw the arrival of two 36ft Leopards with 49-seat Harrington Cavalier bodies. Nos 1743/4 (8743/4 CD) were similar in appearance to their shorter brethren but had an extra window on each side.

In 1963 a new make of body entered the Southdown fleet. Mounted on the 36ft Leopard chassis, this was the Plaxton Panorama, a design which had evolved over a number of years and which had become increasingly popular. Nos 1175-90 (175-9 DCD, 480 DUF, BUF 81-90C) were 49-seaters, except for 1180 which seated only 35, this coach replacing 1129 on tours operated for the Swedish firm of Linjebuss. They were to a quite restrained and not unattractive design but were spoilt by a rather miserable-looking fish-mouth grille. Another 34 Leopards, again with Plaxton Panorama bodies, arrived in 1966, these being 49-seaters numbered 1191-1224 (EUF 191-224D). Cars 1181 onwards were to a revised body style which featured a lot of heavy bright-work around the front and the foremost side windows. 1225-49 (LCD 225-49F), again with Plaxton bodywork, followed in 1968. They were to the same design as the previous batch but lacked the heavier embellishments.

In between the Plaxtons came a further 10 Leopards with Harrington Grenadier bodies, this time seating 41 for Beacon Tours. The arrival of 1754-63 (BUF 154-63C) in 1965 was something of a sad occasion, as they had the last Harrington bodies to be supplied, the coachbuilder ceasing activities following this delivery. The elegant Grenadier and Cavalier designs could hardly be bettered and provided a fitting end to the long line of handsome vehicles that had been built for Southdown over the years.

A further 25 41-seaters were delivered in 1967 and were numbered 1774-98 (HCD 374-98E). They carried Duple Commander bodies, which had a rather angular and not very attractive front end, and were poor successors to the Cavaliers.

The last Harrington bodies were followed in 1970/1 by the last touring coaches to be supplied to the Company. Mounted on Leopard chassis, the first 20 — 1800-19 (RUF 800-19H) — carried Duple Commander IV bodies, which had a much neater appearance than the previous Duple products and looked well in Southdown's two shades of green. These were followed by 25 with Plaxton Panorama Elite bodies which were more restrained than the previous Plaxton coaches. Nos 1820-44 (UUF 320-44J) were the last coaches to be delivered in Southdown green. Both Duple and Plaxton bodywork seated just 32, and these two batches were noteworthy in having sliding vents fitted to their panoramic windows. Many more Leopards were purchased with either Plaxton or Duple bodywork, but all arrived in NBC white or dual-purpose green and white, so we shall leave the story here, when Southdown coaches were something to be proud of and still had that famous Southdown sparkle.

The Leyland Leopard, meanwhile, had been making steady inroads into the stage carriage fleet. The early 1960s saw a steady decline in passenger loadings and operators were frantically trying to find ways to cut expenditure. One-man operation (as it was then known) was an obvious answer, and many rural routes were already being operated on a pay-as-you-enter basis. One-man double-deckers had not yet been legalised, but 1961 had seen the maximum legal length of single-deckers increased to 36ft and this enabled a saloon to carry in excess of 50 passengers — only marginally fewer than a rear-entrance double-decker.

Southdown, like many other operators, began to convert the more lightly trafficked double-deck routes to one-person single-deck operation. The vehicles chosen for the job were Leyland Leopards with 36ft bodies to BET design, a total of 135 being delivered from 1963 to 1968. Apart from livery and seat moquette there was little to distinguish these buses from hundreds being delivered to BET operators all over the country, the only real concession being the 'V'-shaped moulding beneath the windscreen.

The first batch of Leopard buses continued the numbering sequence used for the Tiger Cubs. Nos 665-89 (265-89 AUF) had the standard BET double-curvature windscreen and peaked front dome but retained the normal curved dome at the rear. The next batch started a new numbering sequence, being 100-19 (100-19 CUF). These and all subsequent deliveries had wrap-around windows and peaked domes at the rear. The 1965 batch arrived as 120-39 (BUF 120-39C), again with Marshall bodywork, but in 1966 Weymann was chosen to body 140-59 (EUF 140-59D), these being some of the last bodies built before the firm's Addlestone works was destroyed by fire. 1967 marked a return to Marshall for 160-94 (HUF 760-9E, KCD 170-94F), but the final batch received Willowbrook bodies and arrived as 195-209 (KUF 195-209F) in 1968. (An identical Willowbrook body was fitted later the same year to coach 1224, which had been severely damaged in an accident; this vehicle became No 480 in bus form.) There was little to distinguish between the Marshall and Weymann products, but the Willowbrook examples were easily identified by the lack of the 'V'-shaped moulding, the beading beneath the windscreen being horizontal.

Internally, too, the BET Leopards were very much standard products. They had the usual Southdown moquette but the seats were of basic design, not the shaped frames used on double-deckers of the time. Seatbacks and side panels were in light-coloured Formica. The first two batches had seats for 51, but subsequent deliveries were 45-seaters to meet Trade Union requirements, this being the maximum capacity then allowed for an OMO single-decker. They were put to work on most of the inland routes, replacing double-deckers in many instances.

The final delivery of Leopard buses showed a return to Southdown individuality — probably the last. They were bodied by Northern Counties to an unusual design then unique to Southdown and were fitted out as dual-purpose vehicles, receiving an equally unusual livery of apple green with dark green waistband. The front end was more or less to standard BET design but the main body was at a much higher level and the rear end was Northern Counties rather than BET. Inside, they were well up to usual Southdown standards, with coach seats and wood-grain Formica side panels. They were delivered in two batches and, rather strangely, numbered in the 400-series used by the convertible PD3s, as 450-79 (NUF 450-9G, PUF 160-79H). They were extremely comfortable vehicles in which to ride, and were worthy of being the last single-decker buses on Leyland Leopard chassis to enter the Southdown fleet.

The Weymann-bodied Leopard buses were delivered with fixed windows and forced-air ventilation, which necessitated an air intake beneath the windscreen. the system was not 100% effective, and they were later fitted with one sliding vent on each side, these being taken from the CUF-registered batch. Car 145 (EUF 145D) is seen before modification, at Haywards Heath bus station. *Southdown Enthusiasts' Club*

9. ODD MEN OUT

Despite its affair with Guy, Southdown's love for Leyland double-deckers never faltered. In the single-deck field, however, it was much more fickle, having a number of flirtations with various manufacturers.

Countless odd types were taken over with various operators during the 'Twenties and 'Thirties — far too many to detail here. One fleet that is worthy of mention, however, is Tramocar of Worthing. This forward-looking little company had built up a fleet of Shelvoke & Drewry Freighters, a chassis intended for dustcarts and the like, which had very small wheels and a low floor-height — a feature much appreciated by the town's elderly residents. Sixty years on, the Dennis Dart has offered them the same features! Eleven vehicles were taken over in 1938, but two more were on order and were delivered direct to Southdown. T16/7 (FCD 16/7) were particularly advanced in having rear engines and full-fronted centre-entrance Harrington bodies that bore a strong resemblance to the bodies built for the side-engined AEC Q-type. These useful little buses were obviously way ahead of their time, and, like so many innovative designs,

had a very short working life, being withdrawn by Southdown after a mere four years.

Two more single-deckers were ordered by Southdown for Tramocar services, but instead of favouring Shelvoke & Drewry the order went to Dennis Bros of Guildford, which turned out a low-loading version of the Falcon. Once again these had Harrington centre-entrance bodies, this time seating 30, and were of conventional front-engined half-cab layout. Nos 80/1 (FUF 180/1) were delivered in 1939 for Worthing services, but in 1950 were transferred to Hayling Island. 80 was withdrawn in 1956, 81 soldiering on until 1958.

Throughout the late 'Forties and 'Fifties the petrol-engined Bedford OB with 29-seat Duple Vista body was the favourite workhorse of the country's independent operators, being used on both coach and stage-carriage work. It was hardly the kind of vehicle one would expect to find in the Southdown fleet, but two were purchased in 1948 especially for the Hayling Island– London express service, weight restrictions on Langstone Bridge again being responsible for their choice. Southdown specified a lower than normal seating capacity of 27, and Nos 70/1 (JCD 370/1) looked very smart in the Company's colours, but the gearbox whine and creaking springs were quite out of place in the coach fleet. They were transferred away from Hayling Island when the bridge was rebuilt, 70 being used for a time on bus work in East Grinstead.

The first single-decker buses to be delivered after the war were not Leylands, as might have been expected, but 10 Dennis Falcons with 30-seat lightweight bodies built by Dennis itself. They were basically similar to the Falcons purchased for Tramocar services but had rear entrances. Once again, Hayling Island was their destination, and Langstone Bridge the reason for their purchase. Nos 82-91 (JUF 82-91) spent their entire lives on the island, being withdrawn in 1958.

Since the end of the World War 2, Beadle of Dartford had become something of a specialist in building integral vehicles, working initially with Sentinel and moving on to the coaches built using prewar running units already mentioned. In the mid 'Fifties Beadle introduced its Rochester design, which utilised the Commer TS3 two-stroke three-cylinder engine, a very economical but also a very noisy unit. Bearing in mind Southdown's long association with Beadle, it was not surprising that the Company should take some of the new integrals. Five were delivered in 1956 with centre-entrance 41-seat bodies. As one might expect, their appearance was

This view in London's Victoria Coach Station features a Southdown all-Leyland Royal Tiger, to the left, and a Leyland Cheetah behind No 71 (JCD 371), one of a pair of Bedfords with Duple bodywork for duties from Hayling Island.
Southdown Enthusiasts' Club

Car 86 (JUF 86) was an all-Dennis product purchased specifically for services to/from Hayling Island, where a weak bridge from the mainland made small, lightweight buses essential. Seen *en route* from Havant, 86 was based on the Falcon chassis, which was popular with a number of operators, chiefly for rural routes.
Eric Surfleet / Glyn Kraemer-Johnson collection

not dissimilar to the bodies on Tiger Cub chassis being delivered at the same time, but they had a straighter roof and waistline. Starting a new series, they were numbered 1-5 (RUF 101-5), and spent most of their lives on the London–Brighton express service. A further 20 arrived as 6-25 (TCD 6-15, TUF 16-25) in 1957, shortly before the Beadle factory closed. Basically similar to the first batch, these had front entrances incorporating a 'D'-shaped upper part to the door, with a corresponding curve on the foremost side window. They were sent to work on express services throughout the Company's area. There was no doubt when a Beadle-Commer was approaching, the exhaust sounding like a bucketful of wasps. You either loved or loathed them, but you couldn't ignore them! They gave good service until their withdrawal in 1968/9.

Southdown must have been pleased with its Beadle-Commers, for, following the closure of Beadle's coachworks, it placed in service 45 Commer Avengers which used the same two-stroke TS3 engine. The first batch of 15 arrived in 1959 and had 35-seat bodies by Burlingham. The original Burlingham Seagull body was one of the all-time classics, but when mounted on the Commer front-engined chassis it lost much of the elegance and symmetry it had when built on an underfloor-engined coach. Numbered 26-40 (VUF 926-40), they were never very happy vehicles and seemed to spend much of their time tucked away in dark corners of garages. Most were withdrawn and sold after only eight years' service.

1960 saw a further 15 Commers delivered as 41-55 (XUF 41-55), with another 15 following in 1962 as 56-70 (56-70 AUF). All received Harrington Crusader 35-seat bodywork. Like the Burlinghams, these were not up to their coachbuilder's usual standard, bearing little resemblance to the Cavalier. Their protruding front grilles showed traces of the garish Wayfarer

No 8 (TCD 8), a 1957 Beadle-Commer TS3, rounds the corner in Horsham Carfax, Worthing-bound when almost new. The Carfax is the centre of Horsham where Southdown buses would meet with those of London Transport and Aldershot & District, as well as independent operators. *Eric Surfleet / Glyn Kraemer-Johnson collection*

bodies of the early 'Fifties, while the inward-sloping rear pillar was reminiscent of the contemporary Ford Anglia car. The Crusaders were used mainly on excursion and private-hire work. These, too, only lasted between nine and 12 years, all having gone by the end of 1972.

Before the last Leopard buses were delivered, a new chassis manufacturer had been introduced to the fleet. This was Bristol Commercial Vehicles, which since 1948 had been allowed to sell its products only to the nationalised Tilling group companies. In 1962 Bristol had introduced its RE rear-engined single-decker, which was rapidly proving itself to be the only really successful vehicle of its type. Now it was available on the open market and was being snapped up by operators from all sections of the industry.

The bus version of the RE chassis was available in two lengths: the RESL, which was 33ft in length, and the RELL, of 36ft. Southdown's first order was for no fewer than 40 of the short RESL type with Gardner 6HLW engines. Numbered 210-49 (KUF 210-49F), they had Marshall 45-seat bodies which were much the same as those fitted to the Leopards. The main identification feature was the radiator grille on the front dash, which incidentally left no room for the usual 'V'-shaped moulding. They were fitted with Auster Rotavents on all of the four main side windows.

1969 saw the arrival of 20 of the longer RELL, again with Gardner engines and Marshall bodywork, although the latter seated 49. Strangely, they took fleetnumbers 430-49 (NUF 430-49G), which preceded the dual-purpose Leopards. In appearance they were virtually the same as the RESLs but with an additional half-bay at the rear and hopper vents instead of the not very successful Rotavents.

The following year's order reverted to RESLs, 10 being delivered with Marshall 45-seat bodies, numbered 481-90 (TCD 481-90J) and one with dual-door ECW body having capacity for 37 seated and 28 standing, numbered 600 (TCD 600J). All had Leyland O.680 engines, which made them very nippy little buses; Brighton's allocation of the Marshall-bodied examples was put to work on service 38, previously operated by Brighton, Hove & District Lodekkas, and known unofficially as 'the racetrack'. No 600 was one of a trio, the other two being delivered to the Brighton, Hove & District fleet, now under Southdown control. However, union agreement

could not be reached regarding the operation of dual-door buses, and 600 was eventually repainted red and transferred to BH&D. It was the only example of a vehicle being repainted from green to red.

Three more ECW-bodied REs followed in 1971 as 601-3 (UCD 601-3J), these being of the longer RELL type, again with Leyland engines. However, like the Bristol VRs which were now entering the fleet, they were standard ECW vehicles, only their seat moquette being to Southdown specification and not really true Southdown vehicles at all.

When production of the Leyland PD3 ceased one would have expected Southdown to turn to the Leyland Atlantean, probably with Northern Counties bodywork. One would have been wrong! True, Northern Counties bodies were chosen, but the chassis was the Atlantean's main rival, the Daimler Fleetline. Two batches of 33ft dual-door examples were ordered by Southdown but were delivered to the BH&D fleet. Southdown itself took 15 30ft 71-seaters, these arriving in 1970 as 370-84 (TCD 370-84J). The bodywork was very similar to that on the 'Panoramic' PD3s, with wrap-around front upper-deck window and large side windows fitted with hopper vents. Again, the 30ft body seemed too short to take the panoramic windows, the BH&D 33-footers

No 34 (VUF 934), a 1959 Burlingham-bodied Commer TS3, stands plying for customers at the boundary of Brighton and Hove. The bulbous coachwork never quite seemed to suit the Commer, and looked far better on a heavyweight chassis. The Regency buildings in the background still look grand — more than can be said for Embassy Court (to the right), which has never blended with the Georgian architecture. *W. J. Haynes / Southdown Enthusiasts' Club*

48

looking much sleeker. Inside, both
Southdown and BH&D examples were
well up to Southdown standards, with
'shaped' seats and wood-grain Formica
on seat-backs and side panels. Gardner
6LX engines were fitted. A second batch
in Southdown livery was delivered in
1972 as 385-99 (XUF 385-99K), these
having ECW bodies and, like the second
batch of BH&D Fleetlines, Leyland
O.680 engines, which seemed to make
them much faster. The ECW bodies,
although attractive, were again to ECW's
normal standard, with only the moquette
being to Southdown specification.
Nevertheless, they were extremely
comfortable vehicles in which to ride.
The Northern Counties Fleetlines were
never popular with drivers, it being claimed
that the steering was too heavy. They were
all eventually allocated to West Sussex
depots, being used on local services.

Along with the ECW batch, all were sold
to Crosville in 1980, a number being later
converted to open-top. (Indeed, two
returned to Brighton in 1998 and operated
the open-top service to Devil's Dyke.)

Following the Fleetlines, the standard
fare became Bristol VRTs and Leyland
Nationals to National Bus Company
standards and virtually identical to
hundreds of others all over the country.
True, the earlier, flat-fronted VRs had been
delivered in green cream, and some even
had Southdown moquette, but it was not
long before the traditional colours gave
way to leaf green and white (or just plain
leaf green, in some cases), and the years
that followed are probably best forgotten.
Far better to remember the TDs and PD2s,
the immaculate touring coaches, the open-
top Guys and, of course, the inimitable
'Queen Marys' — all with the sparkle that
marked Southdown's 'Glory Days'.

Open-top Brush-bodied Leyland Titan TD1 No 813 (UF 4813) represented early preservation by Southdown Motor Services, emerging in the early 1960s resplendent in original livery. On this occasion, in May 1974, 813 was about to take up duty on a Southdown Enthusiasts' Club tour to mark the passing of the last cream ex-BH&D Bristol Lodekka. Gone are the days when one could buy a pint of Brickwood's ale! *John Bishop*

49

This rare view depicts 192 (EUF 192), a new Leyland TD5 with lowbridge Beadle bodywork, parked at Pool Valley, Brighton, soon after delivery in 1938. The extent of the lining-out along the roof and beading will be noted; also the six-bay construction, with the small window by the (rear) staircase. Just in view in the background is a Brighton Corporation tram parked in the Old Steine.
Hugh Beck collection

Car 1179 (DUF 179) is no stranger to the rally scene these days, having returned after a long absence. A Leyland Tiger TS7 with 32-seat Harrington coachwork, it is seen on Madeira Drive at the end of an early London–Brighton HCVC run, representing a return to its old operating area when it would be seen on the seafront plying for custom. The plush seating offered, with plenty of legroom, provides a marked contrast with today's coaching.
Malcolm Keeping

51

Leyland Titan 257 (GCD 357) represented a large intake of prewar double-deck buses lasting into the early 1960s. No 257 was a TD5 delivered in 1939 and rebodied postwar by Northern Counties, and is seen at Henfield near journey's end. The screen has been partially blanked-off where the route number once was. Today, a mini-roundabout and road signs 'clutter' this location, adding the feeling of a loss of tranquillity. No 257 was withdrawn very soon after this view was taken. *Malcolm Keeping*

The Guy Arab delivered in the war years introduced a new chassis to the fleet quite by default. The type is exemplified by 458 (GUF 158), with one of the less austere designs by Northern Counties. Seen in the early 1960s on the seafront at Worthing, 458 would soon be withdrawn from service. *John Bishop*

Seldom did the registration number of a Southdown bus fail to match its fleetnumber, but Guy Arab 401 (GCD 975) was one such vehicle. Originally delivered with Northern Counties lowbridge bodywork, it was rebodied in 1951 with a body removed from a prewar Leyland Titan. Here it basks in the sun at Worthing. *Malcolm Keeping.*

The utility Guy Arabs, with their angular bodywork, were obvious candidates for open-top conversion. Seen on the 102 *en route* for Brighton, Park Royal-bodied 446 (GUF 146) represents one of the earlier conversions. These always looked more refined than the later efforts, with the beading running the full length of the body and then finished with scroll coach-style fleetname. *Malcolm Keeping*

Arab 421 (GUF 121), seen at Devil's Dyke with a 'lazy screen' for route 27, depicts the later type of conversion with Northern Counties bodywork. A goodly load of passengers waits aboard for the return journey to Brighton outside the Devil's Dyke Hotel, which is unrecognisable today. The fashions and the Standard car date this view to 1963; the following year, 'Queen Mary' Leyland PD3s would take over such duties. *John Bishop*.

No selection of photographs of open-toppers would be complete without a view of a Guy Arab at the Top of Beachy Head. The Beachy Head Hotel in the background has long since been demolished to make way for a modern building, and the same might, alas, be said of Park Royal-bodied 412 (GUF 72). The advertisement on the bus extols the virtues of route 197 to Birling Gap, another beauty spot steadily disappearing into the sea due to coastal erosion. *Malcolm Keeping*

Out with the old and in with the new! Numerically the last utility Guy Arab, 499 (GUF 399) is seen alongside newly delivered Leyland PD3 413 (413 DCD) at Moulsecoomb depot, Brighton. Many vehicles would pay their last respects at this depot before receiving a 'Private' black-on-white paper sticker and going off 'up north' for sale.
Malcolm Keeping

Double-deck buses would often be cascaded as service vehicles. Such a fate befell the former 461 (GUF 161), which became a tree-lopper. Southdown would always carry out a very professional job in every respect and this conversion was no exception with the beading picked out in dark green and destination covered over. It is seen at Upper Horsebridge, near Hailsham. *Malcolm Keeping*

It is hard to believe this scene at Patcham, Brighton, is the main London–Brighton A23 road. On a bright sunny day in the early 1960s, Northern Counties-bodied Guy Arab 502 (JCD 502) of 1948 vintage is seen at the terminus of route 13, meeting with a Brighton, Hove & District Bristol KSW6G. No 502 was exhibited at the 1948 Commercial Motor Show. *Malcolm Keeping*

In 1946 25 Leyland Titan PD1s were delivered with relaxed-specification Park Royal bodies. The former 267 and 271 (GUF 667/71) are seen in full Southdown livery in the ownership of Mexborough & Swinton, which took a number of Southdown vehicles in the 1960s. Note each has the standard 'Private' paper sticker in the destination screen. *John Bishop*

The halcyon days of the 1960s, when rear-loading buses reversed into Pool Valley, Brighton to depart at regular intervals for all corners of Sussex. No 301 (HCD 901) an all-Leyland PD1 of 1947, waits to depart on route 10 to Arundel. Alongside, 801 (RUF 201), an East Lancs-bodied Leyland PD2/12 will also set off westwards, to Portsmouth on the trunk route 31. *John Bishop*

Inset: In 1958, for the princely sum of 1s 6d (7½p), one could buy a Southdown timetable which would cover all the Company's operations in Sussex. For years the cover remained the same, depicting a Park Royal-bodied Leyland Titan PD1 on the trunk route (12) from Eastbourne to Brighton.

1948 saw an influx of 80 all-Leyland PD2/1s which were very similar to those delivered in 1947. Southdown would improve these vehicles quite noticeably by the provision of triple route numbers above the destination screen. No 339 (JCD 39) is seen so treated on Worthing seafront on route 1 to Pulborough. Showing at the (since refurbished) Dome Cinema was *Doctor in Distress*, starring Dirk Bogarde. *Malcolm Keeping*

'Three for the price of one!' Uckfield suffers a blizzard in the winter of 1963, as an unidentified London-bound Leopard/Harrington encounters Leyland PD2/East Lancs 790 (RUF 190), headed for Haywards Heath on route 80. On the far right, all-Leyland PD2 325 (JCD 25) is Eastbourne-bound on the long 92 route from East Grinstead. The Southdown staff in the foreground appear to be pondering whether it is worth continuing in such conditions. *Malcolm Keeping*.

63

The late 1940s saw the advent of the full-fronted double-deck coach, as introduced by Ribble Motor Services and Birch Bros of London. Southdown 700 (KUF 700) was delivered in 1950 to fulfil the desire for double-deck coach travel between London and Eastbourne. Although 700 was not in itself a success, the Leyland PD2/12 chassis would become the standard for Southdown in years to come, while the Northern Counties body hinted at the style of the later 'Queen Marys'. Relegated to school duties in later days, 700 still looked smart with scroll fleetname when seen at Bognor Regis in the mid-1960s.
Malcolm Keeping

By the time this photograph was taken at Uckfield bus station in 1963, the 'KUF' Leyland PD2s had been replaced on main trunk services by 'Queen Mary' PD3s. No 704 (KUF 704) is seen on the 89A Scaynes Hill route with a very cold driver in full winter Southdown uniform. *Malcolm Keeping*

▲ Brighton's Pool Valley bus station forms the backdrop to this nearside view of 748 (MCD 748), an all-Leyland PD2/12 ready to depart on the 22 to Midhurst. On the right is 1537 (MCD 537), an East Lancs-bodied Leyland Royal Tiger. *Dave Brown*

Petersfield garage is the setting for 772 (OCD 772), a Park Royal-bodied Leyland Titan PD2/12. This bus went on to see further service as a driver-training vehicle in NBC days, and is thankfully preserved for future generations to enjoy the halcyon days of Southdown's half-cab era. *John Bishop*

2 3869

SOUTHDOWN
MOTOR SERVICES LTD

CHEAP
RETURN **5/9** THROUGH
TICKET

**ALTON to
FAREHAM**

This portion to be exchanged on HANTS. & DORSET bus for a Return Ticket WICKHAM to FAREHAM

2 3869

This portion to be retained for RETURN JOURNEY by SOUTHDOWN bus from WICKHAM to ALTON

Williamson, Printer, Ashton
821

Southdown returned to Park Royal for the bodywork on the 1955 batch of Guy Arabs. No 514 (OUF 514) stands in Pool Valley, Brighton, with destination blind set for the longer inland route (25) from Eastbourne via Lewes. *Malcolm Keeping*

An offside view of Guy Arab 553 (PUF 653) showing the classic lines of the Park Royal body. The similarity to London's RT family is not hard to see, despite the five-bay window structure. Southdown's practice of placing registration plates in differing positions from those specified and fitted by most operators is apparent from the blank piece of metal at the bottom of the radiator. *Dave Brown*

Having rebodied a sizeable proportion of Southdown's prewar double-deck fleet in the period 1947-50, Beadle thereafter built very few double-deck bodies. Despite Southdown's allegiance to this company, only 12 more were delivered, in 1956 on the inevitable PD2/12 chassis. Seen at Uckfield, 783 (RUF 183) later became a treclopper, thus outlasting all other members of its class in Southdown service.
Malcolm Keeping

The East Lancs-bodied Leyland PD2/12 with exposed radiator was arguably the all-time classic bus. No 791 (RUF 191) shows off its handsome lines in Tonbridge, Kent, with many miles still to go before reaching Brighton on a hot June day in 1969. *Dave Brown*

In the 1960s and early '70s Brighton's Race Hill would provide much of interest for the coach enthusiast, such as this Duple-bodied Leyland Royal Tiger, 1805 (LCD 205). Dating from 1951, this batch was originally numbered in the 800 series and used on touring work for Southdown's Luxury Tours programme. With only 26 seats in a two-plus-one arrangement, these coaches provided the total comfort which was a hallmark of Southdown Motor Services. *Malcolm Keeping*

▲ This early-1960s view of 1816 (LUF 816) shows that the glory has not been lost since the touring days of the 1950s, when this coach was new as No 816, although the seating capacity has subsequently been increased from the original 26 to 41 for private-hire and excursion work. The stylish coachwork was very much a home-grown product, being built by Thomas Harrington of Hove, whose old premises were sadly demolished recently to make way for PC World. Such is progress! *Malcolm Keeping*

▲ Car 1613 (LUF 613), a Duple-bodied Leyland Royal Tiger, stands on the seafront at Worthing. Fitted with 41 seats, these coaches were used on excursions as well as express services radiating from Victoria Coach Station to Hampshire and Sussex. Behind can be seen an all-Leyland PD2/12 on route 9. *Malcolm Keeping*

▲ Basking in the sunshine on Worthing seafront is an all-Leyland Royal Tiger, 1641 (LUF 641). Dating from 1952, the design represented a very bold step by Leyland Motors, being very angular compared with other products then being marketed, but not unattractive. Several of this type were later down-classed for stage-carriage work, being fitted with destination screens. Here, however, 1641 awaits customers for its 'Mystery Drive', including, presumably, the two ladies standing next to it! *Malcolm Keeping*

▲ May 1963 saw Southdown purchase the business of Buck's Coaches of Worthing and repaint Leyland Royal Tigers 1832/3 into Buck's livery to continue the good name. No 1833 (OUF 833), with stylish 41-seat Harrington coachwork, is seen on the seafront, with a classic Austin Devon Countryman behind. New in 1955 as 26-seaters for tours work, these Royal Tigers were among Southdown's last, for all future Leyland coach deliveries up until 1961 would be based on the lighter Tiger Cub chassis. *Malcolm Keeping*

No 1523 (MCD 523) was one of a batch of East Lancs-bodied Leyland Royal Tigers which could be found in all parts of the Southdown area. This view was taken at Chichester bus station, with a substantial flint wall as the backdrop. Delivery of this class was in two batches in 1952 and 1953, the latter featuring centre entrances. Conversion by Southdown to front-entrance not only enhanced the appearance but also dispensed with the need for a conductor.
Malcolm Keeping

In the late 1950s and early 1960s the dark green beading disappeared from the double-deck fleet and the dark green roofs from single-deckers. No 622 (MUF 622), a Nudd Bros & Lockyer-bodied Leyland Tiger Cub, still sported a dark green roof when seen in the early 1960s at Haywards Heath bus station. Southdown vacated the bus station in the early 'Eighties, and buses now use on-street stops to lay over.
Malcolm Keeping

Much has been written about Southdown's Commer TS3 coaches, which when delivered seemed such a retrograde step for the Company. TS3 stood for 'two-stroke three-cylinder', and when well maintained gave very dependable service. No 4 (RUF 104) was delivered in 1956 with Beadle coachwork; the similarity to that builder's products on Tiger Cubs is evident in this nearside view on Brighton seafront. Harrington and Burlingham would body later examples. *Malcolm Keeping*

Car 1124 (UCD 124), a Beadle-bodied Tiger Cub of 1958, was one of the last of 130 examples of this type delivered. The first, registered in the OUF series, had arrived in 1955 with centre entrances, and would be the new standard for the coaching arm of Southdown Motor Services. No 1124 is seen on a very frosty morning on the Brighton seafront. A feature long gone from Brighton are the Edlins Bars, such as the building in the background. *Malcolm Keeping*

▲ Car 1154 (8154 CD), a Weymann Fanfare-bodied Leyland Tiger Cub dating from 1962, stands at Freshfield Road garage in Brighton. During the winter months this was the ideal spot to find those coaches one normally would not see; they would be serviced, cleaned and parked in the road for the eagle-eyed enthusiasts! The Fanfare was very much a BET product, to which Southdown turned once Beadle had closed its doors.
Malcolm Keeping

Southdown's first Leyland PD3s, with full-fronted Northern Counties bodywork, were delivered in 1958. Given the nickname 'Queen Mary', the type became the standard Southdown double-decker for the 1960s, and in this respect is a classic in its own right. This offside view of 1961 delivery 900 (2900 CD) approaching Rottingdean shows the lines off to full advantage. *Malcolm Keeping*

In the early 1970s spiralling costs and falling passenger numbers forced operators to turn to the overall advertisement bus as a means of earning extra revenue. Although retaining its identity, Southdown had by this time become a subsidiary of the National Bus Company and so 'fell under the spell'. Thus we see a view of 915 (6915 CD) at the rear of Bognor Regis bus station in a scheme for Roberts Off Licences. Around the yard can be seen other 'Queen Marys', a Daimler Fleetline and a Plaxton-bodied Leyland Leopard. The bus station has since disappeared, as has said off-licence chain. *John Bishop*

Uckfield's bus station used to be in the High Street, and is the location for this view of Marshall-bodied Leyland Tiger Cub 657 (7657 CD) and Leopard 682 (282 AUF). The latter would be one of 32 of its type transferred in the early 1970s for service with the East Kent Road Car Co. What was the 92 route is currently operated in two sections by Metrobus of Orpington. *Malcolm Keeping*

Each year Southdown Motor Services would enter a coach in the British Coach Rally at Brighton, and 1963 was no exception, that year's entry being this Weymann Castilian-bodied Leyland Leopard, 1160 (160 AUF). In this view it looks every inch a winner, with the livery enhancing the coachwork. *John Bishop*

In 1964 Southdown turned to another supplier for its coach bodies, going to Plaxton of Scarborough. The Leopard was now the standard Leyland chassis and in 1965 10 were delivered with this fine body style complete with brightwork; the previous year's Plaxton coaches had appeared less attractive, with much less embellishment. Car 1190 (BUF 90C), numerically the last of its batch, is seen at Chichester garage in 1965. *John Bishop*

Storrington, near Worthing, is the setting for this view of 257 (BUF 257C). The bodywork was basically similar to that on the rest of the PD3s except for the curved windscreen. Delivered in 1965, 257 was one of two PD3s fitted with experimental heating and cooling systems, the other being 315 delivered the following year. Neither proved reliable in service.
Malcolm Keeping

◀ Seen at Rottingdean, having travelled from Eastbourne, 365 (HCD 365E) illustrates the change in bodywork design of the final batch of 'Queen Marys' delivered in 1967 and soon known as the 'Panoramics'. Their large windows and small vents soon made passengers very hot, and, to overcome this, 'push-out' vents taken from covertible open-toppers were fitted in the front domes.
Malcolm Keeping

85

Duple's Commander was chosen as the bodywork for the 25 Leyland Leopard coaches delivered in 1967. To my eyes these always looked rather angular, although still fit to wear the Southdown livery! No 1789 (HCD 389E) awaits passengers on the seafront at Eastbourne in 1973. Gone are the days when lines of coaches would stand tempting holidaymakers for a 'spin' through the rich countryside around Eastbourne. *John Bishop*

▲ Like the 'Queen Mary' double-deckers, the BET Federation-style Leyland Leopards seemed to be delivered in a constant stream. Various bodywork was fitted, such as Willowbrook, Weymann and, as here, Marshall. No 162 (HUF 762E) at Haywards Heath bus station is enhanced by the addition of 'bumpers', although these were clearly for decoration only! *Malcolm Keeping*

In the late 1960s it was a surprise to witness the intake of Bristol RE single-deck buses, especially with standard BET-style Marshall bodywork. No 223 (KUF 223F) is seen in the yard at the back of Bognor Regis bus station during the summer of 1973. *John Bishop*

1968 saw the delivery of a further batch of Plaxton-bodied Leyland Leopards which appeared less attractive than the two previous batches delivered in 1965/6. These later vehicles were devoid of the attractive beading and brightwork, and furthermore the dark green paintwork at the base, which so enhanced the vehicle. No 1244 (LCD 244F) is seen on the seafront at Brighton. *Malcolm Keeping*

On a fine, sunny day in 1973, Cavendish Place depot, Eastbourne, provides the setting for this offside view of 471 (PUF 171H), a Leyland Leopard with Northern Counties dual-purpose body. The blinds are set for service 25 to Brighton via Lewes, which lends this view a vintage feel, the route having long since been withdrawn. A Weymann Castilian-bodied Leopard coach lurks behind the 'DP', which is in its short-lived original livery of apple green with dark green waistband. *John Bishop*

▲ Further Duple-bodied Leopards arrived in 1970, these having the updated Commander IV body style. They had very handsome lines, and the golden days of Southdown appeared to be back with a very attractive application of livery. In NBC days vehicles were frequently transferred between fleets, and 1801 (RUF 801H), seen in 1973 on the seafront at Eastbourne, was one of five from this batch which passed to Alder Valley in 1975. The huge crane in the background was in use on the construction of the new TUC building, now an Eastbourne landmark. *John Bishop*

The last coaches delivered in traditional Southdown livery were 25 Plaxton Panorama Elite-bodied Leopards new in 1971. Fittingly, in the early 'Eighties this proud fleet was allowed to paint a number of the batch back into traditional livery, and 1831 (UUF 331J) is seen still plying for customers on Brighton seafront in August 1981 (note the discreet NBC badge). *John Bishop*

Seen on the 203 route in Worthing when brand new is Northern Counties-bodied Daimler Fleetline 377 (TCD 377J). Delivered in 1970, this represented a new chassis type, albeit combined with bodywork from a familiar supplier. Nearly three decades later, two of this class would return to Sussex for a season as open-top buses in Brighton with Metrobus. *Alan Snatt*

While the 1972 deliveries continued to feature Daimler Fleetlines, Southdown was now very much under NBC influence, inasmuch as the bodies were constructed by Eastern Coach Works. Although they looked plain at the front, the apple green and dark green wheels still lent the type that traditional feel. The small, gold 'block' fleetname was a shortlived style introduced by Southdown and superseded by the standard NBC style later in 1972. No 388 (XUF 388K) is seen on local Brighton route 111 to Lower Bevendean, having just turned off the main Lewes Road at Moulsecoomb.

Malcolm Keeping

◄ Seen at Pool Valley, Brighton, are a brace of Bristol VRs — a type that would see many years of service with Southdown and its successors. On the left is 503 (SCD 503H) of 1970 (one of a batch ordered by BH&D), and on the right 511 (UUF 111J) of 1971. With traditional large fleet-name and no advertisements, 511 looks 'right' on the 119 to Tunbridge Wells. *John Bishop*

Southdown as many would like to remember it: Pool Valley in the 1950s. *From a painting by Glyn Kraemer-Johnson*

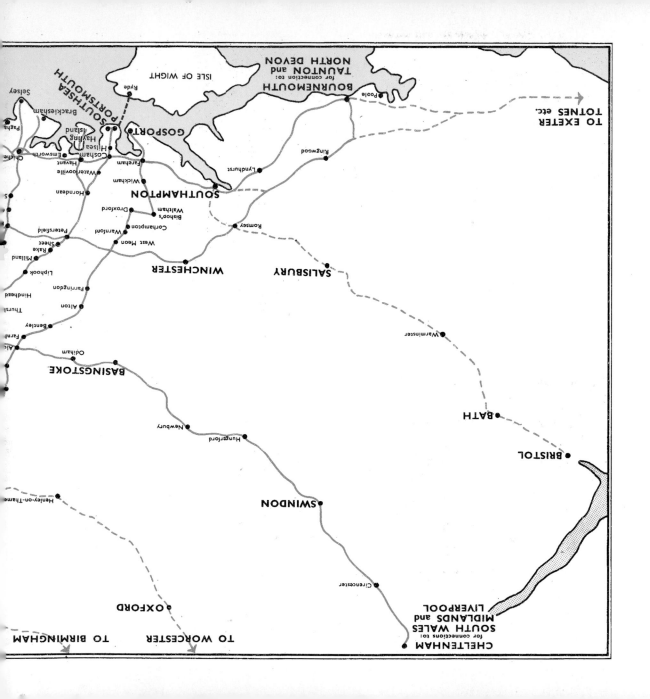